From Site to Sight
Anthropology, Photography, and the Power of Imagery

Melissa Banta
and
Curtis M. Hinsley

From Site to Sight
Anthropology, Photography, and the Power of Imagery

A photographic exhibition from the collections of the
Peabody Museum of Archaeology and Ethnology
and the Department of Anthropology, Harvard University

Melissa Banta and Curtis M. Hinsley
with the assistance of
Joan Kathryn O'Donnell

Peabody Museum Press, Cambridge, Massachusetts
Distributed by Harvard University Press

"From Site to Sight," the exhibition and catalogue, was made possible with funds from the National Endowment for the Humanities and the Polaroid Foundation. The exhibition opens at the Peabody Museum on September 5, 1986, and will travel on a nationwide tour through the Smithsonian Institution Traveling Exhibition Service.

Each caption identifies the earliest generation of photographic image available for reproduction. All negatives, unless described as being glass-plate, are on film base.

Copyright information pertaining to individual images can be found in the photographic index.
ISBN 0-87365-809-4
Library of Congress Catalog Card Number 86-70321

Photography by Hillel Burger
Design by Logowitz + Moore Associates
Editing by Joan Kathryn O'Donnell
Production supervision by Robyn Sweesy
Composition by DEKR Corporation
Printing by Reynolds-DeWalt Printing, Inc.
Binding by Bay State Bindery

Cover illustration
Photographed by J. T. Zealy, 1850, commissioned by Louis Agassiz
Daguerreotype
Renty, an African-born slave, South Carolina

Frontispiece illustration
Photographer unknown, ca. 1890s
Albumen print
Edward H. Thompson and native "guide,"
Yucatán, Mexico

Contents

Photographer unknown, 1892–1893
Albumen print
Peabody Museum Second Honduras Expedition,
Copán

The Honduras expeditions were among the first research expeditions sponsored by the Peabody Museum. Under the challenging field conditions of the Central American jungle, George Byron Gordon (left) and an assistant improvised a cumbersome but ingenious camera setup. Like other early archaeological investigators, Gordon was not trained in anthropology or photography; he joined the expedition as its surveyor. Nevertheless, he appreciated the importance of visual records and used the camera extensively during his excavations.

Foreword

From the moment of its invention, photography has been utilized to serve and advance scientific inquiry. Anthropologists were quick to adopt the new technology in their efforts to record and interpret the evolution, variation, and achievements of humanity. Today anthropologists exploit virtually all known photographic techniques in order to understand better our shared past and present. In a way that no other medium can, photography recreates the history of anthropology and reveals the often volatile relationship between anthropologist, photographer, and subject. The emphasis of this exhibition and catalogue is on the still photograph and its impact on anthropological interpretation. The anthropological uses of motion picture film deserve separate treatment, though they share with the still photograph similar issues of usage, interpretation, and meaning.

With the invention of the camera, the public came to accept photographs as vivid witnesses to "reality." All too frequently, however, anthropologists and photographers were influenced by their own preconceptions and prejudices, presenting in their images stereotypical attitudes and portraying societies or individuals as depersonalized cultural artifacts. But in the late nineteenth and early twentieth centuries, tribal cultures began to assert their own influence over Western thought and aesthetics, as the recent Museum of Modern Art exhibition, "'Primitivism' in 20th Century Art: Affinity of the Tribal and the Modern," so powerfully demonstrated (Rubin 1984). At the same time, images of non-Western peoples began to take on a more sympathetic appearance, and the "native" became romanticized and lionized in photographic work like that of Edward S. Curtis and Gertrude Kasebier. Over the years both the photographer's imagery and the anthropologist's vision have changed. In the early days of anthropology and photography, various strains of social evolutionism dominated intellectual circles. Today Claude Lévi-Strauss's structural anthropology considers Western cultures no farther advanced than tribal societies; in his view tribal cultures are merely different, with forms of logic comparable to scientific thought.

Since its founding in 1866, the Peabody Museum of Archaeology and Ethnology at Harvard University has acquired a significant photographic collection documenting the fieldwork and research undertaken by the museum and by anthropologists and photographers of other institutions. Photographs taken on anthropological expeditions document people, sites, environments, methods of exploration, and discoveries in the field. The archives also includes studio views of artifacts from the museum's collections. The museum's Photographic Archives makes this important collection of over half a million images accessible to a worldwide scholarly and public community. These photographs illustrate museum catalogues, textbooks, slide, film, and videotape presentations, periodicals, scholarly publications, and exhibitions.

Even before the turn of the century, the museum collected and stored photographs. Systematic care, cataloguing, and preservation of the collection is, however, a far more recent undertaking. The Photographic Archives was officially established in 1976 with the support of a farsighted grant awarded by the National Science Foundation. Daniel W. Jones, Jr., photographic archivist, saw his task clearly: "The first order of business was to properly care for, identify, and make accessible this invaluable collection." As a result of his vision, the Photographic Archives today has constructed a cold/dry storage vault, one of the first to be installed in this country, to prevent fading of the museum's color images and motion picture film. It has developed an innovative system for converting nitrate images, which deteriorate with time, to safety film. The archives also houses an excellent studio facility in which the staff photographer, Hillel Burger, creates fine made-to-order images of the photographic collection and museum objects. Finally, the Photographic Archives has developed a computerized documentation system, one of the first of its kind, for storage and retrieval of information pertaining to the collection. These accomplishments represent pioneering efforts and, as intended by the National Science Foundation, have served as a model for other institutions across the country that have recognized the need to modernize their own photographic archives.

The Peabody Museum's exhibition galleries were closed from 1981 to 1984 while the museum undertook an extensive storage renovation project for its collections. Unable to exhibit on its own premises during that time, the museum instituted Collection-Sharing, a large-scale loan program for collaborative exhibition to allow its collections to be seen nationwide. Recently, an exhibition program of both temporary and permanent installations has been developed for the museum's galleries. "From Site to Sight" inaugurates the reopening of the museum's exhibition areas by presenting a broad view of the uses of photography in the discipline of anthropology. Many of these photographic collections have never before been publicly exhibited. We are particularly pleased to feature this exhibition as part of the festivities related to the 350th year of the foundation of Harvard College. It is fitting on this anniversary that the oldest ethnological and archaeological museum in the nation should trace the past and present accomplishments and perspectives of anthropology.

The Peabody Museum is grateful to the National Endowment for the Humanities for its generous support of this exhibition and catalogue; to the Smithsonian Institution Traveling Exhibition Service (SITES) for making the exhibition available to museums throughout the country; and to the Polaroid Foundation for its donation of film supplies on behalf of the project.

Melissa Banta, director of the Photographic Archives at the Peabody Museum, developed and very effectively guided this program from inception to completion. Special thanks go to Curtis M. Hinsley, cultural historian at Colgate University, who, with Ms. Banta, has sensitively explored the uses and abuses to which the power of the photographic image can be put. Lea S. McChesney, administrator of exhibitions, once again has expended great effort to ensure that a major museum collection receives the public exposure it deserves.

Since its founding, the Peabody Museum has attempted to foster a cross-cultural appreciation of the human condition. It must be admitted that the realization of our intentions has not always borne positive results. Even once-accepted professional terminology appears biased or derogatory on reexamination. What used to be called "primitive" society is no longer regarded as such. "Primitive" may seem a clearly derogatory term, but anthropologists also have come to view with suspicion even such an apparently neutral designation as "tribal" society. If past images, whether written or photographed, were permeated by attitudes of colonialist superiority, racism, or the idealized notion of the innate nobility of the "savage," what then of our present perspective? We first must admit to the sad reality that earlier biases maintain a tenacious hold on significant segments of the population. It is doubtful, however, that more recent attitudes, some of them forms of neo-romanticism, are entirely credible. Some present the builders of Stonehenge as highly adept mathematician-astronomers, or shamans as practitioners of "science," or the !Kung hunter-gatherers of Africa as the original affluent society. Others celebrate the presumed demographic and ecological balance of earlier or simpler societies. But these may be no more than our own wishful projections onto other peoples, past and present, in an effort to ameliorate the problems of our own day.

Historically, anthropologists and photographers have shared a certain perspective. Both have focused on humans—whether an entire culture as presented in an anthropological account or a single photographic subject as arrested on film—as *objects* of study and interpretation. In today's global village, threatened by potential extinction, the nature of our study must shift from objectifying others to understanding ourselves and our interrelations with others. Only this approach will allow for the continued existence of the whole.

C. C. Lamberg-Karlovsky
Director
Peabody Museum of Archaeology and Ethnology
Harvard University
Cambridge, Massachusetts

Acknowledgments

In following the path of the photographic record in anthropology, we have drawn upon a wealth of collections and knowledge. We deeply appreciate the contributions of those individuals who have made this collaborative effort possible.

The exhibition and catalogue were generously supported by the National Endowment for the Humanities, the Polaroid Foundation, and the Colgate University Research Council. The Smithsonian Institution Traveling Exhibition Service coordinated the exhibition's nationwide tour, and special thanks are due to Eileen Rose.

We were fortunate to work with a team of talented and creative consultants who were responsible for design and production: Charlie McMillan and his staff at the McMillan Group and Norman Clark for the exhibition; Joe Moore and his staff at Logowitz + Moore Associates for the catalogue; and Eric Harrington, who matted and framed all images for the exhibition.

It was with the guidance and enthusiastic support of C. C. Lamberg-Karlovsky, director of the Peabody Museum, and Garth Bawden, former assistant director, that "From Site to Sight" was carried through. Our deep gratitude goes to Lea S. McChesney, administrator of exhibitions, for kind encouragement and for effectively overseeing this project from beginning to end. Robyn Sweesy, editor of the Publications Department, supervised the catalogue production, offering continual support and assistance to the authors. The exhibition and catalogue are graced with the photographic work of Hillel Burger, who created original images and fine reproductions of archival collections. Paula Chandoha and Christopher Burnett provided assistance in the production of some of the images. Daniel W. Jones, Jr., photographic archivist, as always generously shared his expertise and knowledge. Donna M. Dickerson, of the Publications Department, offered a valuable perspective on the exhibition label copy. Linton Watts and Barbara Isaac of the Photographic Archives, Victoria Swerdlow, Una MacDowell, Laura Ventresca Montgomery, and Kathleen Skelly of the Collections Department, Madeleine W. Fang and Barbara J. Mangum of the Conservation Department, and many other staff members and volunteers devoted their energy to this project. The staff of the Tozzer Library kindly made their rich collections available to us.

We are indebted to the members of Harvard University's Department of Anthropology and to the photographers, scholars, and curators who shared their time, collections, and research experience. They generously aided us in tracing developments in photography and anthropology, past to present. We gratefully acknowledge the contributions of Marie J. Adams, Thomas Barfield, John Barry, Garth Bawden, Thomas Wight Beale, A. Kay Behrensmeyer, Jeffrey P. Brain, Ian W. Brown, Glenn Conroy, William Crawford, Irven DeVore, Nancy DeVore, Cora Du Bois, Michael Geselowitz, Robert Gardner, Ian Graham, James Guimond, William W. Howells, David Kolody, Ira Jacknis, C. C. Lamberg-Karlovsky, Robert Maddin, Yvonne Maracle, Joan Mark, Alexander Marshack, David Maybury-Lewis, Pia Maybury-Lewis, John F. Merkel, Jack Naylor, Gorm Pedersen, David Pilbeam, Mark Solomon, Nancy Schmidt, Michael Vannier, Evon Z. Vogt, Steven Ward, Peter S. Wells, Donna Wilker, Gordon R. Willey, Stephen Williams, and Paul Wing. Margaret B. Blackman graciously contributed the introduction to the catalogue and provided valuable criticism of the manuscript.

Numerous archives and publishing companies cordially furnished us with images. We thank the American Museum of Natural History, Boston *Globe*, Curtis Publishing Company, EOSAT Company, George Eastman House, Harvard Cabot Science Library, Harvard Film Study Center, Harvard Semitic Museum, Harvard Widener Library, Louisiana Office of State Parks, Macmillan Journals Limited, Musée du Louvre, National Geographic Society, Time Incorporated, United States Department of the Interior, and Yale University Press.

Above all, Joan Kathryn O'Donnell has assisted us in every respect. We are especially grateful for her help in the exhibition production, her excellent research and editing, and her many fine ideas.

Harrison W. Smith, 1911
Gelatin dry-plate negative
Complete darkroom in a suitcase for processing
photographic plates in the difficult field conditions
of the tropics

"A suitcase...formed the body of the dark-room. The right half is occupied by a water-tight rubber bag, supported on three sides by the suit-case and on the fourth by a brass rod, which may be seen extending over the edge of the case and hooked into the lock. The developing tank, filled with developer at a temperature sufficiently below the normal to allow for rise of temperature before developing begins, rests in this rubber bag, as shown. The object of the rubber bag is to prevent damage to plate-holders that are placed in the other half of the suit-case in the event of the tank spilling over" (Smith 1911:953).

Harrison W. Smith, 1911
Gelatin dry-plate negative
The suitcase-darkroom in use

"Two long sleeves permit the operator to transfer the plates from the holders to the tank without the necessity of himself being in the confinement of a darkroom, a distinct convenience in the tropics, even on the rare occasions when a darkroom is available" (Smith 1911:953).

Introduction

A . . . potent use of visual records of vanishing ways of life is as a source of information on man and how he has responded and developed over time in different settings, and under different conditions. Such information, by increasing our understanding of our own species and its possible modes of response and adaptation, can contribute uniquely to an increasing and cumulative self-understanding as we adapt into the unfolding future.

E. Richard Sorenson, 1975
"Visual Records, Human Knowledge, and the Future"

"From Site to Sight" is a special exhibition. Unlike most photography exhibitions, it presents its images not strictly as art, social documentary, or even history. "From Site to Sight" is about the "culture of imaging." Visually and in words it explores the changing patterns of belief and behavior brought to making, viewing, and understanding photographic images within the context of anthropology. The Peabody Museum's collection of more than five hundred thousand visual documents is an appropriate one through which to trace major trends in the anthropological use of photography: the assembling of visual data for a racial typology of the world's peoples in the nineteenth century; the recording of noncollectible native architecture and art in the field; the serial photographing of behavior and ritual; the photographing of scenes and activities to serve as illustrations in expositions and museum exhibitions; the documenting of excavations and their artifacts; the illustrating of professional publications; and the popularizing of anthropology through visual images. The exhibition also traces the anthropological use of photographic technology from the mid-nineteenth-century daguerreotype through the cumbersome and fragile glass plates of the turn of the century to today's familiar 35mm roll film and instant photography. In the late twentieth century anthropologists also have embraced the less familiar technologies of microphotography,

aerial stereophotography, photogrammetry, infrared photography, and satellite imagery. Overall, the images in "From Site to Sight" are witness to the evolution of the discipline of anthropology, reflections of our changing views of the human condition.

Behind the multitude of specific purposes to which photography has been put in anthropology is an underlying conviction that the photograph is capable of extending the fieldworker's powers of observation and understanding. The photograph is a means of visualizing words, a recorder of information not otherwise obtainable, a scientific document of powerful authority. Though long ago we intellectually acknowledged that the photograph does not mirror truth, over the years its use as field tool and illustration has reflected the interests and supported the hypotheses of the anthropologist/image maker. The many stark portraits of native peoples made by photographers from the mid-nineteenth to the early twentieth centuries were prompted by a view of humanity as divisible into racial types on the basis of physical appearance. Daguerreotypes of African-born slaves in America taken in the 1850s under the direction of natural historian Louis Agassiz were used as visual support for the existence of biologically distinct groups. Alice Fletcher's commissioned photographs of the Omaha even more consciously reflected a particular reality; they were designed as proof of the Omaha's strides toward "civilization." Contemporary anthropologists similarly direct their cameras toward their own fields of interest, and always the image has as much to say about its maker as its subject.

Anthropological photography also holds a mirror to the history of native cultures. Through the photograph, we see their transformation from tribal entities to subject peoples within nation-states and, now, fourth-world societies seeking self-determination and perpetuation of cultural distinctiveness. It has been an enormous journey. Just one hundred years ago, a photographer on a polar expedition made the first photographs of Iñupiat people and settlements in the vicinity of what is now Barrow, Alaska.

Today, Iñupiat students attending a multi-million-dollar high school in Barrow take courses in photography and video. And, as anthropology turns its attention to the service of native peoples, some of these same students participate in an archaeological and oral history field school in which they learn about the Iñupiat past by putting to service the hundred-year-old photographs of their culture (Gerlach, Blackman, and Hall 1985). In many parts of the world the native is as likely as the anthropologist to use a camera, as I discovered when photographed by a Nikon-toting Native Canadian on the same reserve where, as an anthropologist, I had taken many photographs over the years. (I have often wondered what became of my image. Like so many powerless native subjects who have faced the image maker, I was never offered a copy.) Within native communities today, amateur photography may be little different from photography in any other rural community, serving to record family members, life crises, and other events. At the same time, more serious native photographers are creating what they see as distinctive visions of their own cultures. The pioneering work of seven Hopi photographers published in *Hopi Photographers, Hopi Images* (Masayesva and Younger 1983) is a case in point.

As the field of visual anthropology took form in the 1960s and 1970s—building on the photographic endeavors of Margaret Mead, Gregory Bateson, John Collier, Sol Worth, and others—photography assumed more than an adjunct role to the discipline and became a focus of anthropological study. Mead and Bateson pioneered the use of still photographs as a primary route to the investigation of culture. Over a two-year period in Bali, they made and documented twenty-five thousand images. In "an experimental innovation" in the presentation of culture, they published 759 of these photographs in thematically related groups augmented by text (Bateson and Mead 1942). Mead and Bateson's work tackled head-on a major difficulty faced by anthropologists in using what John Collier calls the "bouquet of culture" presented by a still photograph. "The common experience has

been that this photographic conglomeration defies validation by the controlled systems by which other humanistic data can be evaluated. When this uncontrollability is discovered, the tendency is not to use photographic data" (Collier 1967:64). This could explain why Mead and Bateson's work, after nearly fifty years, stands as a unique enterprise.

The difficulties of which Collier writes are intensified when photographic research focuses on historical images. Wrenched from their cultural and temporal contexts, they present an even greater challenge to the researcher. Yet anthropologists today are increasingly realizing the richness of the photographic record and have turned to the systematic study of archival collections. Aided by the endeavors of photohistorians, their efforts have included documentation of works by individual photographers (Glenn 1981, 1983; Gidley 1979); investigation of images of particular ethnic groups (Scherer 1981a; Longo 1980; Younger 1983); study of the issue of inaccuracy in historical photographs (Scherer 1975b); examination of the anthropologist as image maker (Jacknis 1984); exploration of the relationship between photographer and native (Blackman 1982a); reconstruction of archaeological sites through photoarchaeology (Gavin 1985; Rockett 1983); and, finally, discussion of the potential of "photographic ethnohistory" (Blackman 1981).

In the world's archives, hundreds of thousands of historical photographs of ethnographic, archaeological, and physical anthropological value await investigation. The problems of their study lie not just in the uncontrollable wealth of information present in the images themselves but in their wide distribution in scattered locations (at universities, museums, historical associations, etc.), the inaccessibility of some archival images, and, not least of all, the expense of researching such materials firsthand. The study of photographs of Subarctic Indians, for example, could lead the researcher to nearly forty archives, in such far-flung localities as Whitehorse, Austin, Berkeley, and Washington, D.C.

Alexander Marshack, 1973
Ultraviolet photograph
Cave painting of horse, Niaux, France

How and when did human beings begin to make symbolic representations of their world? For the past twenty years, Alexander Marshack, research associate of the Peabody Museum and author of *The Roots of Civilization* (1972), has studied the Ice Age art of Cro-Magnon peoples of Europe. In his search for the thoughts expressed thirty thousand years ago, Marshack combines microscopic analysis with close-up photography, utilizing both ultraviolet and infrared photographs to bring out details of artifacts, engravings, and cave paintings and reveal information about their manufacture, use, and processes of deterioration. The green and yellow fluorescence seen below indicates organisms that have destroyed painted portions of the image and restores details of the horse's muzzle line, whiskers, and neck muscles that cannot be seen under normal light (right).

Some archives contain well-catalogued, cross-referenced images, while others are still in need of basic documentation (Scherer 1981b). Some of the researcher's problems are eased by useful directories to photographic collections such as *Picture Sources 4*, published by the Special Libraries Association (Robl 1983), and the recently compiled directory to all photographic holdings within Harvard University (Harvard University Library 1984).

Improvements in technology have allowed new methods of photodocumentation in the field (portable video equipment, for example), while new technology assists in making the vast archival holdings of historical images available to the researcher and provides the means to organize that information. To make their collections more accessible a few archives have put portions of their photographic holdings on microfiche. The Smithsonian Institution, for example, has published five thousand microfiche images of Native Americans from the National Anthropological Archives (Viola 1974). The Alaska State Library has microfiched eight thousand of its ninety thousand photographs. This microfiche collection has been deposited in libraries throughout the state and is available to individuals and outside libraries for purchase (Alaska 1981).

Computer technology has also facilitated access to the information-rich content of photographs. User-friendly database management programs for microcomputers allow the researcher to organize and manipulate information from large samples of photographs. Using such a program on a recent study of 143 studio photographs of British Columbia Indians made in the 1860s, I was able to tabulate the ethnic identity of individuals, their style of dress, pose, the use of photographer's props, as well as information on date and photographer. I was able then to sort this information in a variety of ways, a feat impossible by simply relying on notetaking and visual memory (Blackman 1986). The Peabody Museum has implemented a computerized documentation system for its photographic collections, the creation of which involved developing cataloguing guidelines for photographic material, standardizing terminology for anthropological subjects, and implementing a database management program to organize and retrieve information (Banta 1980). In the future, photographic archives may make images available to researchers on videodiscs (Earle 1981). One wonders, given the new technology, how the twenty-five thousand images that Bateson and Mead laboriously pored over might now be put to the service of anthropology.

The images shown here, like other archival photographs, are a permanent record. They can be viewed from something approximating the original perspective of their makers, understood reflexively as part of the fabric of anthropology at the time of their making, and reviewed again and again by untold future researchers. The magical, modest photographic image, handmaiden to anthropological research, window to the development of anthropology and to the culture history of myriad societies, is deservedly honored in "From Site to Sight."

Margaret B. Blackman
Department of Anthropology
State University of New York
College at Brockport

Photographer unknown, ca. 1898
Albumen print
Studio photograph of tattooed man, Marquesas
Islands, Polynesia

16

Inuit

Kwakiutl

Sioux

Crow Missouri

Ponca

Penobscot

Omaha
Ohio Mounds

Shoshone Colorado
Hampton Institute

Navajo
Mississippi

Santo Domingo
Columbia, South Carolina

Ohio

Lower Mississippi Valley

Caddo

Rio Grande
Chichén Itzá

Zuñi
Labná

Pecos

Chitimacha

Zinacantan
Maya

Palenque

Yaxchilán
Coclé

Copán

Sitio Conte

Manaus

Amazon

Marquesas Islands

Rio das Mortes

Rarotonga

Paracas

Shavante

La Paz

Aymara

From Site to Sight World Map

Historic and Contemporary Culture Areas and
Locations Represented by the Photographs

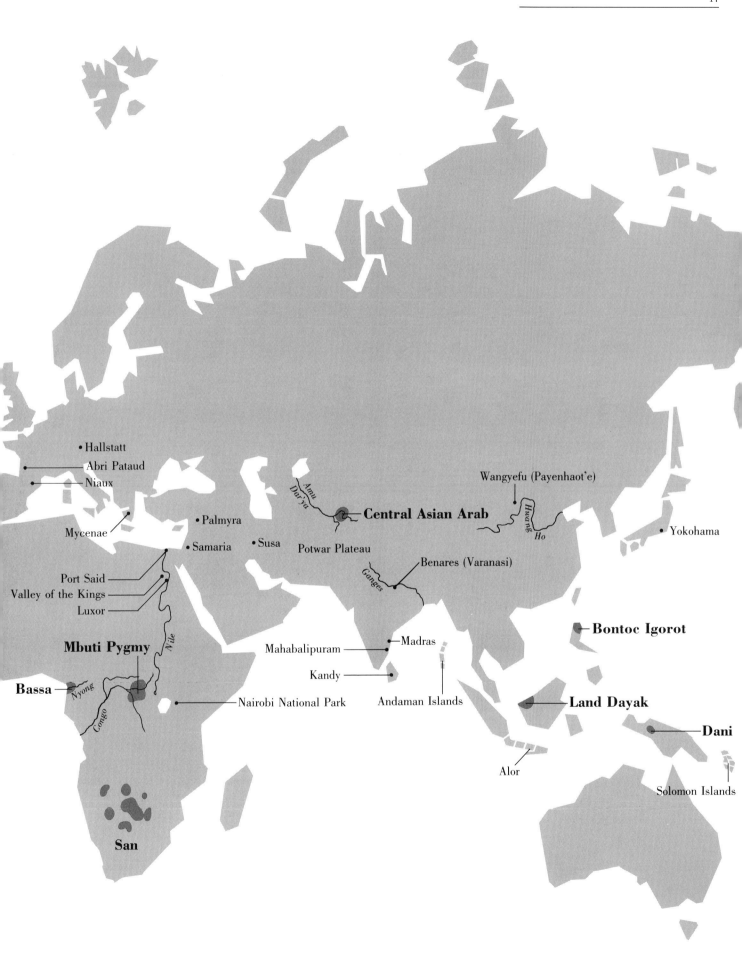

• Hallstatt

Abri Pataud

Niaux

Mycenae

• Palmyra

• Samaria

• Susa

Port Said

Valley of the Kings

Luxor

Mbuti Pygmy

Bassa

Nyong

Congo

Nile

Wangyefu (Payenhaot'e)

Central Asian Arab

Amu Dar'ya

Potwar Plateau

Huang Ho

• Yokohama

Benares (Varanasi)

Ganges

Bontoc Igorot

Mahabalipuram — • Madras

Kandy

Nairobi National Park

Andaman Islands

Land Dayak

Dani

Alor

Solomon Islands

San

1
Photographer unknown, 1904
Gelatin silver print
Bontoc Igorots killing a dog for a feast,
Philippine Reservation, St. Louis Exposition

"An exposition within an exposition" (Rydell 1984:167), the Philippine Reservation at the St. Louis Exposition of 1904 consisted of forty-seven acres on which nearly 1,200 Filipinos lived in several villages. This re-creation was an attempt to illustrate to the American public the islands' rich natural resources and many native types, who had reached varying stages of "civilization."

1 Photography in the Service of Anthropology

"No one would believe it who had not seen it," wrote Christopher Columbus in reference to the generosity and innocence of the native peoples he encountered on his first voyage to the New World (Major 1870:7). Travel and discovery, Columbus soon realized, end finally at home with the effort to transform personal experience into shared public knowledge: "Although others may have spoken or written concerning these countries, it was all mere conjecture" (ibid.:16). This communication problem is at the heart of the anthropological endeavor. The fifth-century B.C. Greek historian and ethnographer Herodotus considered it his first duty "to interpret his picture of humankind; to illustrate parallel cases; to extract by comparison the genuine observation from the blundered folktale commentary" (Myres 1908:122). In the same spirit, anthropologists today gather and interpret data, taking advantage of their ever-increasing ability to communicate by means of visual imagery. And like Herodotus and Columbus, they travel broadly and belong marginally, mediating in time and space between the familiar and the strange, between self and other.

"Anthropology" comes from the Greek *anthropos*, meaning "man," and *logia*, meaning "study." The earliest form of the discipline dates to the civilizations of ancient Greece, Rome, and China, whose explorers—in addition to pursuing new trade routes and resources—recorded their observations about newly discovered lands and peoples. Similar accounts were written throughout the age of European exploration, beginning in the fifteenth century, and during the era of North American expansion in the nineteenth century. By the 1860s, anthropology had emerged as an organized scientific enterprise. Although many other social sciences are concerned with the study of people, anthropology is a unique holistic interpretation of humans, past and present, as cultural and biological beings.

Today's anthropologists belong to a vigorous, multifaceted community of inquiry, divided into many subdisciplines with varying degrees of in-

teraction. Biological or physical anthropologists, concerned with the human being as a physical organism, investigate human evolution, relations to other primates, and comparative anatomy and physiology. They study fossil remains, observe primate behavior, and record variation among living human populations. Like archaeologists, biological anthropologists excavate sites and analyze material remains to make inferences about the life of early man. Teeth, for example, provide information about size and diet, and analysis of skulls can show cranial capacity and its relation to brain size. The comparative study of living primates in the field enables biological anthropologists to develop an improved understanding of similar extinct species. With new techniques of laboratory analysis, genetics has also become an area of anthropological investigation.

Archaeologists study the material remains of the human past, both historic and prehistoric, piecing together accounts of culture change through discovering and excavating sites, deciphering written records, and analyzing artifacts. They examine animal, plant, human, and cultural remains retrieved from locations where earlier societies lived, worked, practiced ceremonies, or buried their dead. Based on these data, inferences can be made about climatic and environmental conditions, social order, means of subsistence, manufacturing techniques, trade, and ritual practices. In effect, the complete excavation of a site results in its final destruction. The archaeologist's work thus involves slow, careful, and detailed recording of each stage of excavation by describing, photographing, and cataloguing the remains. Materials removed from the field are subjected to a variety of laboratory analyses, and their functions and meaning are further identified.

Social and cultural anthropologists, or ethnologists, study contemporary cultures, investigating—among other things—social and political organization, economic systems and subsistence patterns, language, religion, art, and technology. They attempt to understand human society by observing, describing, and then comparing cross-culturally these various cultural patterns. For a period of time social and cultural anthropologists live "in the field" with the people they study, participating in their lifeways and making written accounts of their observations. They rely extensively on native informants or "consultants" for their data. Sound and videotape recordings, still photographs, and motion picture footage enable anthropologists to supplement written description, capturing a wealth of detail for further examination that may have been missed in field observation.

Beneath the disparate activities of virtually all anthropologists lies a common structure of experience: a periodic movement out from the center, or home (metropolis, university, museum), to the anthropological periphery (the site or "the field," which may be on the other side of the globe or in one's own backyard) and back again to the center. Anthropologists still travel a polar universe in search of knowledge. Their basic pattern is temporary immersion in an alien environment followed by return with new knowledge (Slotkin 1974). This is the seasonal ebb and flow of anthropology. Its central distinction is between home (or self) and the field (or other).

In the movement between home and field, then, the anthropologist develops three critical and distinct relationships: to the subjects of study; to other anthropologists; and to larger groups of the lay public. "From Site to Sight" demonstrates that the nature and intensity of these relationships vary with the anthropological terrain of the different subfields but that certain problems are commonly faced. Anthropologists cannot escape the moral complications involved in studying living peoples or the equally compelling questions raised by disturbing the graves and habitations of human ancestors or removing artifacts from their place of origin. However the specific issues differ among anthropology's subdisciplines, two elements are constant in the growth of anthropology as a whole: it involves studying other humans; and it has been conducted until very recently in a context of political domination.

Like all scientists, anthropologists seek to gather reliable data based on their observations. The fact that the anthropologist's subject of scrutiny is human beings creates unsettling dilemmas. It is admittedly more difficult to be objective about people than about any other subject of scientific investigation, even when the contact is indirect, as in examining archaeological artifacts or human remains. Where the study of other peoples is concerned, the subjects have historically been afforded limited opportunity for interpreting, exchanging ideas about, or controlling the uses of cultural information gathered by the anthropologist.

The fundamental core-periphery structure of anthropology has roots deep in the central global-political experience of the past five hundred years: the expansion of nation-states and their economic interests over the rest of the earth. Not surprisingly, anthropology as an approach to understanding humanity has been deeply influenced by these political circumstances. Always there has been a conflict between our desire to gain knowledge about other peoples and their own right to privacy and self-determination. Over the past generation the intrusion of the modern industrial world into even the remotest human societies has complicated an already sensitive endeavor.

But the humanist voice of the discipline was raised at an early point. In 1550, half a century after Columbus's final voyage, Bartolomé de Las Casas and Juan Giné Sepulveda met in Valladolid, Spain, to debate the moral state of the New World aborigines: Were they Aristotle's "natural slaves" or free moral agents? Las Casas, unlike Sepulveda, had lived for years in New Spain and could draw on firsthand experience in arguing against the vicious Spanish slave system. More important, he laid the groundwork for comparative ethnology based on observation and empiricism rather than medieval scholasticism (Pagden 1982). Sepulveda, taking a traditional interpretation of Aristotle, defended the enslavement of New World "barbarians" as not only justifiable but, under the

To transform personal experience into shared public knowledge: this communication problem is at the heart of the anthropological endeavor.

2
Photographer unknown, 1892–1893
Gelatin dry-plate negative
Peabody Museum Second Honduras Expedition, Copán

John G. Owens, astride a mule, led the Peabody's expedition to Copán in its first two seasons (1891–1893) and supervised the transport of molds of stone monuments to the coast for shipment to the museum. Some early explorers proposed to buy entire sites and ship them, stone by stone, to Europe or North America. The logistics of conveying whole monuments by pack mule, oxcart, barge, and ship—or on the backs of porters—made such schemes impractical, and more pragmatic researchers resorted to casting molds of desired antiquities.

3
Photographer unknown, 1899
Gelatin dry-plate negative
Central American room, Peabody Museum

Original stone monuments and molds of stelae from Copán and other Central American sites came to rest here in the museum at Harvard University. Removed from their original setting, these artifacts lose much of their visual power and contextual meaning, making *in situ* photographic documentation even more valuable.

circumstances, obligatory. The debate was inconclusive, however, and the Spanish colonial authorities continued to wage genocidal war. As a result of warfare and introduced disease, perhaps as many as ninety percent of the native population of New Spain were exterminated between A.D. 1500 and 1600 (Nash 1974).

The exhibition "From Site to Sight" is designed with the conviction that the lesson of Las Casas remains pertinent today, for we are still caught in the dilemmas of power. As nuclear physicists discovered forty years ago, scientists who act directly as brokers between their discipline and politics usually lose control of new-found information. Once in the public domain, it can be turned to uses quite different from or contrary to their intentions. Wittingly or not, anthropologists frequently have served the interests of imperial or commercial expansion, particularly the nineteenth-century concepts of manifest destiny and "white man's burden" (Asad 1973; Hinsley 1985). Instances of positive anthropological influence on governmental power over subject peoples have occurred as well; applied and "action" anthropology have existed for many years. Explorer and geologist John Wesley Powell successfully argued to Congress in 1879 that a government-funded Bureau of American Ethnology would provide valuable scientific data to guide Indian reservation policy and save public money. Twenty years later, anthropologist Franz Boas called for an applied science of anthropology to advise public policymakers on issues concerning ethnic groups, including liberalized immigration laws (Hinsley 1981:277; Goldschmidt 1979). For a century American archaeologists have lobbied strenuously and often successfully to preserve prehistoric and historic sites from destruction by developers and vandals.

Without minimizing such efforts, we must recognize that anthropological influence is primarily indirect and operates by slowly altering public opinion. Witness Boas's lifelong crusade against racial bigotry or Margaret Mead's tireless efforts on behalf of humanitarian causes. The anthropologist's relationship to the public has been colored by a traditional skepticism

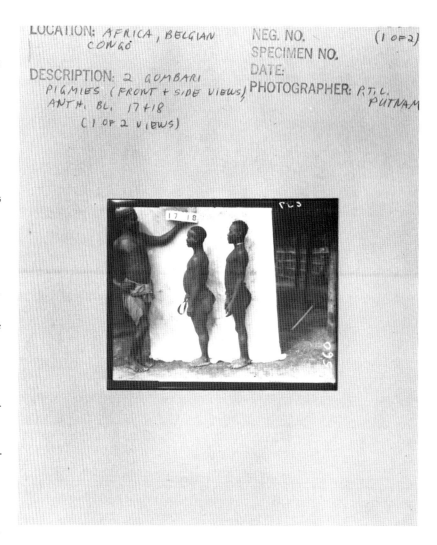

about the usefulness of anthropology as well as by widespread misconceptions about the discipline itself. Yet the relationship is vital to the anthropologist, for public opinion both creates the climate in which work goes forward and provides the forum for evaluating its social implications.

Anthropologists thus function in an uncertain relationship with the peoples they study and the wider public. In the field they are in an ambivalent power relationship, seeking access to information over which their subjects have control yet sometimes capitalizing on unequal social or political status in order to gain that access. At

Photography...compounds the problems of control and interpretation of information.

Photography...compounds the problems of control and interpretation of information.

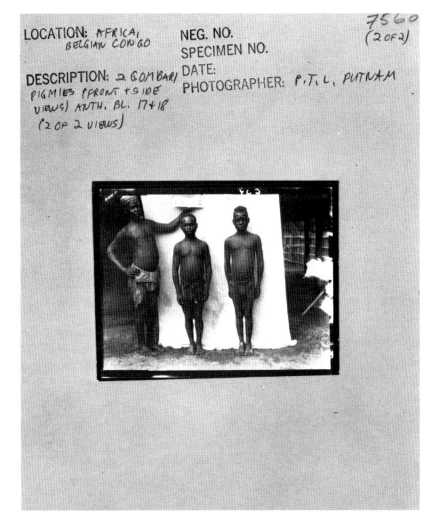

4
Patrick Putnam, ca. 1928
Gelatin silver prints
Mbuti Pygmies, Belgian Congo (Zaire)

Anthropologist Putnam studied and lived among the Mbuti people for over twenty years. His photographic documentation covered a wide variety of subjects, including standard recordings of physical types.

home anthropologists are in sole control of the interpretive process and the product presented to the public. Finally, when that material enters the public domain, anthropologist and subject have very little control over the wider uses and interpretations of the original information.

Photography, one of the tools anthropologists use for their research, compounds the problems of control and interpretation of information. Anthropologists have used the photographic image for research data, for presentation to the professional community, and for public consumption. These distinctions of use are often unclear, however, and images taken for one purpose may ultimately serve another. The objectivity of the anthropological photograph is further compromised by the fact that photographic technology remains bound to the constraints of human intervention. Armed with the camera, anthropologists can probe, scan, magnify, reduce, isolate, contrast, debase, or idealize their subjects. Through photography, they can create, disseminate, and forever seal in time their own interpretations of humankind.

In the mid-nineteenth century, to a culture infatuated with mechanical inventions, photography seemed a clear break from artistry and subjectivity, an alliance with nature on behalf of vis-

5
Michael Rockefeller, 1961
Color transparency
Men and women dance to celebrate killing of an
enemy. New Guinea

In 1961 the Peabody
Museum launched an
expedition to western
New Guinea to record
the life of the Dugum
Dani, a tribe of warrior
agriculturalists. As an
integral part of the
ethnographic study,
filmmaker Robert
Gardner—with Jan T.

Broekhuijse, Eliot
Elisofon, Karl Heider,
Peter Matthiessen,
Samuel Putnam, and
Michael Rockefeller—
richly illustrated in
photographs and on
film the life of the
Dani, then still un-
touched by the indus-
trial world.

ual clarity. The creation of a photograph is, on one level, a chemical-mechanical process, recording on film or paper the rays of light emanating from an object. However, many intervening variables distance the viewer from the subjects of these representations. The technology (type of camera, film, and printing technique) determines what can be recorded and how it will be presented. The resulting image can represent only symbolically the subject's actual shape, texture, dimensions, color, and overall context.

The person behind the camera also intervenes. Within the limits of the available technology, photographers may choose from a wide range of recording and printing options that will affect the final image. The photographer's selection and recording of a particular moment takes it out of its context in the flow of real-life experience and places it in another, possibly unrelated, context. The photographer also can alter the elements of that moment by manipulating the setting, posing the subject of the image before recording it, and later, placing the image next to captions, text, other photographs, or in a particular form of presentation. As an extension of its operator's perceptions, this medium possesses unique properties, making it in many respects more subject to the limitations of human observation than other scientific research tools.

Yet the variables between viewer and subject also create endless opportunities for anthropological research. Photographs can render the exotic familiar, enhance the commonplace, capture movement in time, reveal unseen features, and present remote perspectives. Photographs can illustrate subjects in their original setting, providing important information for fuller understanding. Alternatively, the camera can isolate subjects from their surroundings, affording new interpretations. The image freezes a slice of time, which, unlike life itself, the scientist may analyze again and again. What the camera has recorded may in some instances be all that remains of peoples, places, and their histories.

The photograph remains an ever-changing mirror, reflecting different realities at each viewing. As our understanding of history and peoples changes, the photographic image offers new insights into documented subjects and the attitudes of those behind the camera. With the passage of time we find meanings that transcend the intentions with which an image was originally created. Almost one hundred fifty years after its invention, we are just beginning to realize the generative and sustaining nature of the photograph.

"From Site to Sight" investigates the ways in which anthropologists have used the camera as a recording, analytic, and aesthetic medium and what this body of photographic work reflects about the changing perceptions of these researchers toward their subjects. In hindsight, we can appreciate the contributions of earlier anthropologists while acknowledging the scientific doctrines and cultural biases of their times. As we approach the work of contemporary anthropologists, we should recognize the difficulty in seeing our own biases.

This exhibition illustrates the role of photographic imagery in anthropology from the discipline's formative years to the present, with documentation selected primarily from the Photographic Archives of Harvard University's Peabody Museum of Archaeology and Ethnology and from the work of past and present members of the Department of Anthropology at Harvard University. The Photographic Archives includes research undertaken by the museum since its

founding in 1866 and work done by other anthropologists, photographers, and institutions.
Housing over half a million images, the archives constitutes a remarkable corpus of anthropological photography (Banta 1982).

"From Site to Sight" does not present a comprehensive overview of the history of anthropology,
photography, or the Peabody Museum. Photographs have been selected to examine the potentials and limitations of using the camera as a
fact-gathering and interpretive tool and to explore the broader implications of the uses and
misuses of visual imagery within the human sciences. We have sampled the work of numerous
anthropologists and photographers to illuminate
different aspects of these issues. It is not within
the scope of this exhibition or the Peabody Museum's photographic collection to examine all
the issues involved or to present in its entirety
the work of any individual.

Almost twenty-five years ago a sense of crisis
began to emerge in the discipline of anthropology. "With the withdrawal of the umbrella of
European power that long protected their entry
into the colonial field," historian of anthropology George W. Stocking explains, "anthropologists found it increasingly difficult to gain
access to (as well as ethically more problematic
to study) the non-European 'others' who had traditionally excited the anthropological imagina-
tion—and who seemed finally about to realize,
through cultural change, the long-trumpeted
anthropological prediction of the 'vanishing
primitive'" (Stocking 1983:3–4). Although
Stocking's reference is to ethnography, archaeologists and biological anthropologists also in-
habit a postcolonial world in which rising
national consciousness not only makes field accessibility problematic for non-nationals, but
results in calls for repatriation of collections
previously removed from their country of origin.

Various responses and suggestions for rethink-
ing, redirecting, and reinventing anthropology
have come forth (Hymes 1973), most of which
look toward an enterprise more "reflexive" and
"relevant" to current concerns. After a quarter
century of self-analysis, it is not clear whether
anthropology has solved its problems or simply
gotten over them—or neither. One positive,
permanent legacy of the crisis, however, has
been a serious historical appraisal of anthropology and the firm realization that it cannot be
separated from the larger world in which it has
developed and to which it contributes (cf.
Weaver 1973).

"From Site to Sight" arises from a sense of the
need to continue this critical examination of the
history of anthropology and bring a new perspective to our knowledge about humankind.
Photography plays an important role in this enterprise. By illustrating the richness of human
diversity, it can promote a more profound understanding of and respect for all peoples and
cultures. We hope that this exhibit will encourage scholars and the public to reevaluate the
past, present, and future of anthropology as an
active humanist philosophy. At the close of the
twentieth century, the vision of human commonality and global harmony remains an unrealized
and increasingly urgent goal. As anthropologist
Stanley Diamond has observed (1980:16), anthropology "will either become a partisan of the
people it has hitherto studied—at home and
abroad—and help recreate a society responsive
to human possibilities, or it will become nothing at all."

Throughout this exhibition, the eyes that look
back at us are our own.

Almost one hundred fifty years after its invention, we are just beginning to realize the generative and sustaining nature of the photograph.

6
Robert Gardner, 1961
Black-and-white negative
Mother weeps alone as her child's corpse is laid on a funeral pyre. New Guinea

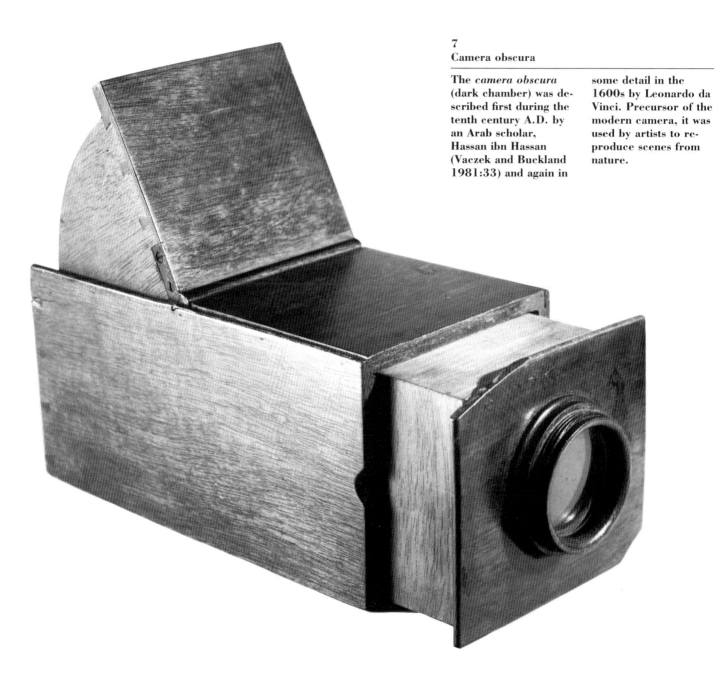

7
Camera obscura

The *camera obscura* (dark chamber) was described first during the tenth century A.D. by an Arab scholar, Hassan ibn Hassan (Vaczek and Buckland 1981:33) and again in some detail in the 1600s by Leonardo da Vinci. Precursor of the modern camera, it was used by artists to reproduce scenes from nature.

Basic Photographic Processes

Photography is a running battle between vision and technology....The [technology] is ornery and obstinate and sees only what it will. As a result, human experiences and natural wonders that the technology is not yet able to see go unrecorded—and even unnoticed. Each time the technology enlarges its sight, our eyes grow wider with surprise.

William Crawford, 1979
The Keepers of Light

The dream of duplicating nature onto a fixed surface is centuries old. In a 1760 novel Charles François Tiphaigne de la Roche described an imaginary process remarkably similar to modern photography (Newhall 1980:13–14):

> *The elementary spirits have studied to fix these transient images....The first effect of the canvas is that of a mirrour; there are seen upon it all the bodies far and near, whose image the light can transmit....the canvas, by means of the viscous matter, retains the images. The mirrour shows the objects exactly; but keeps none; our canvases show them with the same exactness and retains [sic] them all....*
>
> *Survey with thy eyes (said the Prefect), survey the most remarkable events that have shaken the earth and decided the fate of men. Alas! What remains of all these powerful springs, of all these great exploits? The most real signs of them are the traces they have left upon our canvases in forming these pictures.*

Not until the mid-nineteenth century, with the invention of photography, did the dream become a reality.

Photography has involved an ongoing interaction between the nature of the technology and the ambitions of its users. In the field, anthropologists use a variety of means to observe, record, and collect cultural information, preserving the meaning of its original context to increase its interpretive value once removed from the field.

Photography—in the field, laboratory, or studio—can, by immobilizing the elements of time and space, in every sense enhance the anthropologist's results. Over time, developments in photography have increased its simplicity of use, more successfully captured movement and color, and expanded our scope of vision both inwardly and outwardly. These capabilities have sometimes allowed anthropologists to "see" a subject differently, altering their ways of thinking about it. Conversely, changing theoretical approaches in the discipline have led anthropologists to adopt existing photographic techniques to explore those perspectives.

The Camera

Knowledge of basic optical principals dates to Aristotle, who described the phenomenon of seeing the crescent shape of a partially eclipsed sun projected onto the ground through the holes of a sieve. Seventeenth-century artists made use of this phenomenon by means of the *camera obscura*, a darkened chamber that admitted light through a convex lens set in one wall, projecting an inverted image onto the opposite side of the chamber (fig. 7). The photographic camera works on essentially the same principle as the camera obscura. Light is admitted into the darkened chamber of the camera through a converging lens that permits focusing and directs an inverted image onto the surface opposite the lens. There it is recorded on a light-sensitive emulsion that is supported by a base material. Correct exposure requires that the emuslion receive a certain "quantity" of light, either a greater quantity for a shorter duration or a lesser quantity for a longer duration. Cameras therefore have a "shutter," with a range of time intervals for admitting light, and an "iris" in the lens system, which can be set to different diameters to control the intensity of incoming light. Cameras range in complexity and size and can be equipped with a variety of different shutter speeds, apertures, and lenses.

Early cameras consisted of two telescoping boxes for focusing the image and a lens cap that served as a shutter. Metal or glass plates were used to record the image. The difficulty of early processes and unwieldiness of the equipment made photography a trying enterprise (fig. 8). As a result, early anthropologists often relied on professional photographers to record their material. With the introduction of the Kodak camera by George Eastman in 1888 (fig. 9), photography became more accessible to the amateur—and to the anthropologist. The camera was easy to operate, hand-held, and used manufactured roll film. With continued technological improvements, cameras became smaller and exposure times shorter. In 1924 the Leica, the first popular precision 35mm camera, was produced. Its excellent optical quality, compactness, and quiet shutter provided anthropologists with an easy-to-handle, less obtrusive tool for field research. Another camera popular with anthropologists, the Rolleiflex, was developed in 1928. It took 2¼-inch-square pictures and used roll film. In 1947 the Land camera, which used Polaroid film, enabled anthropologists and their subjects to see instantly what had been recorded. Since the development of high-quality and relatively inexpensive Japanese models in the early 1950s, the 35mm camera has been the most popular camera in general use. Other cameras designed for special applications, such as aerial photography and microphotography, have also been adopted for anthropological purposes.

9
Kodak camera, ca. 1888

"You press the button, we do the rest" was the advertising slogan of the first simple-to-use, hand-held camera introduced to the general public. It revolutionized the popularity of amateur photography and brought to anthropological photography a new immediacy and spontaneity.

8
Large box camera (background) and portable photographic laboratory, 1869

The "latest" in American photographic technology, a portable darkroom for collodion wet plates, could be strapped to the back of the peripatetic photographer.

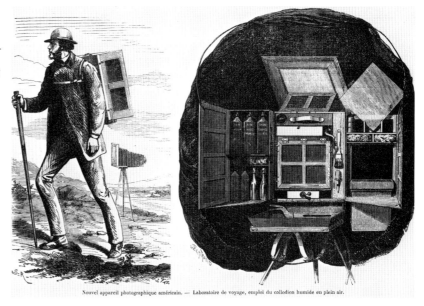

Nouvel appareil photographique américain. — Laboratoire de voyage, emploi du collodion humide en plein air.

The Photographic Image

Traditional photographic processes depend on the light-sensitivity of silver halide crystals (silver-iodide, -bromide, and -chloride), minute particles of which are suspended in an emulsion coated onto a base. Exposed to light reflected from a subject, these compounds are chemically altered. When processed further, they produce a visible image of the subject on the base material. Emulsions used today and in the past have included collodion, albumen, and gelatin, while base materials have included metal, glass, plastics, and paper. Over the years, manufacturers have steadily increased their emulsions' "speed" (sensitivity to light), at the same time improving their grain quality to enhance tonal fidelity.

Once exposed in the camera, black-and-white negative material is immersed in three chemical solutions: a developer to bring out the latent image; a stop bath to halt the developer; and a fixer to make the image permanent. A water wash then removes residual fixer. The processing of color negatives is somewhat more complicated. Both negative and positive images can be produced photographically. In a negative image the camera records onto a film-based emulsion tonal values or colors opposite to those of the subject (light areas of the object appear dark, and dark areas appear light). Positive images reflect the same tonal values or colors as the subject. Positives can be made directly in the camera without the production of a negative ("direct positives") or they can be made from a negative by exposing light-sensitive paper to the negative and processing the image. The many combinations of bases, emulsions, and cameras have produced distinctly different types of photographic imagery.

Black-and-White Processes

The first permanent image produced by a photochemical process was made in France in 1826 by Joseph Nicéphore Niépce, who exposed a sensitized pewter plate in a camera obscura. Later, Louis Jacques Mandé Daguerre, working in partnership with Niépce, improved upon this technique and created the daguerreotype, also a direct-positive process.

Unaware of Niépce's and Daguerre's work, William Henry Fox Talbot in England described the first negative-to-positive process as early as 1835. Known as the calotype or Talbotype, it was the forerunner of the process by which most photographic images are made today. Talbot used paper negatives to make salted paper prints. Their fibrous quality gave the image a very soft appearance. Unlike the daguerreotype, the calotype could be used to produce multiple copies of an image.

Negatives

Glass-Plate Negatives
Glass plates included collodion wet plates and gelatin dry plates (fig. 10). The collodion wet-plate process, introduced in the mid-1850s, used glass coated with collodion, a semiliquid substance that dried on the plate as a tough film, to produce negatives. Prints made from these negatives were less grainy than prints made from paper negatives, but the plates had to be sensitized, exposed, and developed before the collodion dried. Photographers in the field had to transport chemicals, glass plates, and the entire darkroom setup in order to create their images.

Gelatin dry plates were a distinct improvement in photographic technology. They could be purchased already sensitized, had a faster emulsion than wet plates, and, once exposed, could be processed at a later time. Introduced in the 1870s, dry plates greatly increased the mobility and ease of field photography.

Cellulose Nitrate Film
In 1887 Eastman introduced the first successful, flexible plastic support material: cellulose nitrate. Used for roll and sheet films, cellulose nitrate is not fragile like glass plates but is highly flammable and deteriorates with time due to its chemical instability (fig. 11).

Safety Film
Safety film was first used for X-ray photography in 1937 and had supplanted all other negative materials for general use by the 1950s (fig. 12). The base material first used was cellulose acetate, a substance of low flammability. Today cellulose triacetate and polyester films are used.

"It would be well to have a full gross of plates ordered as a certain percentage of damaged and broken plates is always to be expected, especially in this hot, damp, mule-packing land. . . . We shall need the chemicals for fixing and developing as well as the sensitized paper and printing frames to make the proofs. When the surveyor comes down he had better distribute the things among his articles of clothing in his trunks . . . or they may think them of a quantity sufficient to make a charge of duty."

Edward H. Thompson to Charles P. Bowditch
Mérida, Mexico, 14 August 1888

10
Photographer unknown, 1888–1889
Gelatin dry-plate negative and
positive print
Edward H. Thompson at Labná, Mexico

"We are, as you see, . . . among the ruins and so far in a very comfortable and prosperous condition. We have a room . . . in the Palace nicely fitted up for photographic work, tanks, dark room," wrote Thompson to Charles P. Bowditch on

12 December 1888 (Bowditch Papers). Thompson, who spent over forty years exploring the ruins of Yucatán, used the gelatin dry-plate process. His photographic studio/darkroom in an arched chamber at the Maya

site of Labná displays the chemicals and equipment required to create his images. A vast improvement over the collodion wet-plate process, dry plates still challenged the patience and ingenuity of the field photographer.

11
Deteriorating nitrate base negatives in storage album

Cellulose nitrate film inevitably deteriorates, resulting in the complete destruction of the photographic image itself as well as surrounding materials.

12
Hallam L. Movius, Jr., 1958
Black-and-white (safety film) negative and positive print
Excavation of the Abri Pataud, Les Eyzies, France

A multinational team of researchers under the direction of Hallam L. Movius, Jr., of the American School of Prehistoric Research, excavated the Upper Paleolithic rock shelter of Abri Pataud in southwestern France between 1958 and 1964. As in the early days of archaeology, the team was multidisciplined, but rather than gifted amateurs, they were specialized professionals, studying settlement patterns and the paleoenvironment. Members of the archaeological field crew use all the tools of their trade, from trowel to pen to camera.

13
Wilhelm and Friedrich Langenheim, 1848
Daguerreotype
African youth

Covered by protective
glass, daguerreotypes
were usually placed in
leather, wood, or plas-
tic cases. The plates
ranged in size, the most
popular being 2¾
inches by 3¼ inches.
When first introduced,
daguerreotypes had an
exposure time of
twenty to thirty minutes
and were more success-
ful at capturing station-
ary subjects than
human beings. By the
time this image was
made, exposure times
had been reduced to
forty seconds or less.
The sitter for this study
is believed to be the
eighteen-year-old Bush-
man (San) exhibited
before the Academy of
Natural Sciences in
Philadelphia by Dr.
Samuel Morton, a pi-
oneer of biological an-
thropology. The
daguerreotype was ap-
parently collected by
Louis Agassiz, a collab-
orator of Morton's in
the development of the
theory of "special crea-
tions" (American Heri-
tage 1977:110).

Positives

Daguerreotypes

The daguerreotype process, invented by
Daguerre in 1839, utilized a silver-plated cop-
per sheet as a support material. It was sensitized with iodine vapor, exposed immediately,
then developed in mercury vapor. The silver
plate gave the image a beautiful luminous quality without graininess (fig. 13). Depending on
how the plate is held to light, both positive and
negative images of the subject can be seen. The
daguerreotype was difficult to produce and its
lengthy exposure time limited its use to stationary subjects, particularly landscapes, architecture, and portraiture. A direct positive, the
daguerreotype was a unique image and could
not be used to generate duplicates.

Albumen Prints

A variety of paper support materials appeared
in the nineteenth century, but the great majority
of photographs made from the 1850s to the
1890s were printed on albumen paper (fig. 14).
An albumen (egg white) emulsion secured the
photographic image on the surface of the paper
rather than in the paper itself, producing a
glossy, grainless print toned to a rich brown
with gold chloride. Albumen prints tend to fade
and yellow if not properly fixed and stored.

Gelatin Silver Prints

Gelatin silver prints were introduced in England
in 1871 and soon overtook albumen prints in
the market (fig. 15). An improvement over albumen prints, they did not fade or discolor as
readily and required less time to print. Print-
ing-out gelatin papers (with warm brown and
purple tones) required no chemical developing:
the image appeared as a result of being exposed
to strong light. The paper was then toned,
fixed, and washed. This type of paper was later
replaced by developing-out gelatin papers (with
cooler blue and grey tones). These required liq-
uid chemical developers like those used today
to bring out the image.

Instant Photography

Instant photography is another form of direct-
positive imagery (fig. 16). Edwin H. Land developed the Land camera in 1947. It used inte-
grated rolls of film and print paper to create a
positive image in the camera itself. Today both
black-and-white and color instant print films are
in use. Some of the films include a negative
process that allows multiple positive prints to
be made from the original negative.

14
Charles Shepherd and James Robertson, ca. 1895
Albumen print
Indian carriage and pair

The majority of photographs made from the 1850s to the 1890s were printed on albumen paper. Albumen prints were mass-produced in a variety of sizes, from pocket-size miniatures to large folio prints, and mounted on cartes-de-visite (visiting cards), cabinet cards, stereocards, and in full-size albums. Shepherd owned the oldest Anglo-Indian photographic company and in partnership with Robertson (and earlier with Samuel Bourne) was the foremost supplier of photographic views of India to British citizens at home and abroad.

15
Frederick R. Wulsin, 1927
Gelatin silver print
The postmaster (right) in his official regalia with one of the head lamas, Wangyefu (Payenhaot'e), Inner Mongolia, China

Developing-out gelatin papers began to be most widely used around 1910 and remain the most common form of photographic printing paper. They were quickly adopted by travelling photographers like Wulsin, who made an invaluable photographic record of China's northwestern frontier in the 1920s, documenting the ancient societies of Mongolia and Tibet on the threshold of change (Alonso 1979).

16
Ian W. Brown, 1982
Instant black-and-white print
Lookout site, Jefferson County, Mississippi

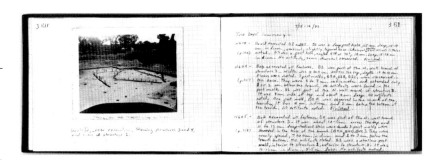

Because prints are available immediately after exposure, instant photography is ideal for field research. Archaeologists on Harvard University's Lower Mississippi Survey use instant photography to document the location of historic and prehistoric sites. The images are mounted in field journals in which detailed information about the survey or excavation is recorded.

Color Processes

Photographers have always wanted to reproduce color. Before a direct color-reproducing photographic process was introduced, photographers colored their images by hand (fig. 17). The Autochrome process, patented in 1904, used starch grains (microscopic in size and colored orange, green, and violet) dispersed on a glass plate, which was then developed as a positive.

In 1935, Eastman Kodak introduced a film that was developed as direct-positive transparencies in a variety of formats (fig. 18). Earlier processes used three separate negatives, each exposed through a different color filter (red, green, or blue) to create one color image. The new film incorporated three color-sensitive materials in one multilayered piece of film. In 1942 the first color-negative process was introduced in this country. Today many color printing processes are in use, including type C prints (from a color negative), Cibachrome prints (from a positive transparency), and dye-transfer prints (from a three-color separation process).

17
Harrison W. Smith, 1912
Hand-colored lantern slide
Land Dayaks, Sarawak, Malaysia

Lantern slides, positive transparencies mounted on glass for projection, were often dyed or hand-painted with watercolors or other transparent pigments. The quality of the color could range from realistic to romantic or even garish. Smith, on the engineering faculty at the Massachusetts Institute of Technology, travelled widely in the South Pacific and eventually retired to a plantation in Tahiti. He prepared an impressive collection of hand-colored transparencies of his travels for lectures and published his images in popular scientific and geographic journals.

18
Hillel Burger, 1980
Color transparency
Embroidered textile, ca. A.D. 800–1200,
Paracas, Peru

Color transparencies, viewed by transmitted light, have a greater range of tones than color prints made on an opaque base and therefore appear to have much richer and more brilliant color quality. Color reproductions such as this photograph of a textile from the north-central coast of Peru often are made from 4-inch-by-5-inch transparencies. The 35mm format provides anthropologists with a valuable teaching tool.

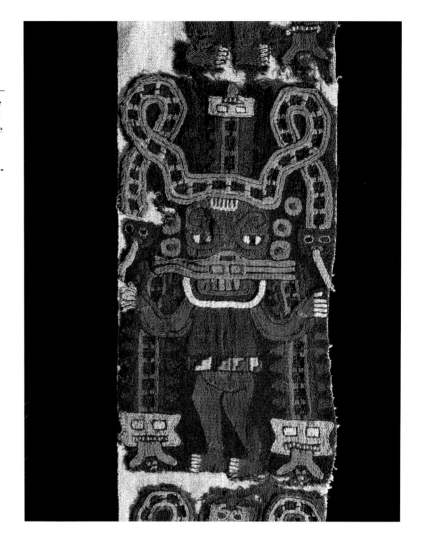

19
Scowen and Company, ca. 1870–1880
Albumen print
Kandian chiefs, Ceylon (Sri Lanka)

The spread of colonial empires and the invention of photography in the mid-nineteenth century made possible the study of peoples and places on a worldwide scale. By the 1870s, commercial photographic studios such as Scowen and Company had been established in every large city in India and Ceylon. Produced for a fiercely competitive tourist trade (Worswick and Embree 1976:9), their photographic records offered Western society a first glimpse of exotic foreign worlds. This photograph of a group of chiefs from Ceylon was collected during a Harvard botanical expedition in the 1880s.

3

Nineteenth-Century Visions of the Exotic:
Travel and Expeditionary Photography

Before . . . progress has completely done its destructive job, before this present which is still the past has forever disappeared, we have tried, so to speak, to fix and immobilize it in a series of photographic views.

Adrien Bonfils, ca. 1898

In the mid-nineteenth century two developments occurred simultaneously: the invention of photography and the emergence of modern anthropology. Technological advances and the growth of colonial empires caused rapid and profound cultural changes for non-Western societies. Yet the expansive age also made possible the study of humankind on a global scale and produced the camera as a means of visually preserving the very traditions it had a hand in altering. The camera did not lend itself to easy use by amateurs until improvements were made in the technology in the late 1880s. Professional photographers under the auspices of governments, scientific expeditions, or commercial studios undertook much of the early photographic documentation of foreign peoples and places (fig. 19). Their subjects—peoples, crafts, street scenes, architecture, and landscapes—were in a broad sense anthropological. Although created for a variety of purposes, the work of professional photographers was widely marketed. Collected by anthropologists as well as by the general public, these images influenced Western perceptions of other peoples and played a role in fostering the discipline of anthropology in its early years.

At the onset of the photographic age, the new technology was hailed as an objective, factual means of visual communication. As the art critic Lady Elizabeth Eastlake wrote in her 1857 essay "Photography," the technology gave "cheap, prompt, and correct facts to the public" (Newhall 1980:93–94):

Photography is the purveyor of such knowledge to the world. She is the sworn witness of everything presented to her view. What are her unerring records in the service of mechanics, engineering, geology, and natural history but facts of the most sterling and stubborn kind?

This revolutionary form of communication produced visual images of astonishing authenticity and furnished striking new representations of non-Western societies. They were as important to their time as photographs transmitted from the outer reaches of space are in ours: without them, the nonspecialist had only a vague concept of these distant realities (Davis 1981:9). "Photographs were not viewed as metaphors of experience, but rather as sections of reality itself. If photographs showed gigantic trees and awe-inspiring mountains, then all the trees were gigantic and all the mountains awe-inspiring. When photographs depicted Indians as 'savages,' Indians were confirmed as savages" (Lyman 1982:29).

From the start, the camera's coverage was global. The first publication of views originally recorded by the camera was *Excursions daguérriennes: Vues et monuments les plus remarquables du globe* (1840–1844). Published by N. P. Lerebours, it contained engravings copied from daguerreotypes taken around the world. In 1852 Maxime Du Camp, working under commission from the French government, published *Égypte, Nubie, Palestine et Syrie*, a series of calotypes of the Middle East that was "the first photographically illustrated travel book" (Vaczek and Buckland 1981:35). Early photographs were presented in a variety of forms, including cartes-de-visite (see fig. 29), stereographs (fig. 20), and hand-colored images (see figs. 17, 24, and 29), bought either individually or bound in albums. Many nineteenth-century travel photographs received wide visibility at world's fairs and expositions.

Knowingly or not, photographers struck a rela-tionship with whatever they recorded, which manifested itself in the final image. The tech-nology of the period—large, imposing cameras, the need to carry cumbersome equipment in the field, long exposure times, and difficulties in processing images—was one factor in determin-ing the nature of this interaction (fig. 21). In-vestigating the possibilities of the medium through composition, exposure, and printing, photographers could make their subjects appear especially inspiring or exotic (fig. 22). The very nature of places and peoples captured by the camera also influenced photographic results. Some subjects invited dramatic presentations. The naturally spectacular Indian landscape (fig. 23) or the samurai warrior's imposing stance (fig. 24) were not easily improved upon or com-promised by the photographer.

20
Timothy O'Sullivan, 1873
Albumen print mounted on stereocard
"Navajo brave and his mother," southwestern
United States

During his relatively short career O'Sullivan worked for commercial studios, carried out his own expeditions in the western territories, and served as a photogra-pher for the United States government. This photograph of a young Navajo man and his mother was taken during Lieutenant George M. Wheeler's 1873 survey of the Southwest. Like the work of other expedi-tionary and travel pho-tographers, many of O'Sullivan's images were mass-produced as stereocards. Conven-tional stereoscopic photographs are twin images taken from points 2½ inches apart, the average distance between the human eyes. A twin-lens cam-era is usually used to make the photographs, which are viewed through an optical de-vice known as a stereo-scope to create a three-dimensional image. After the late 1850s stereophotographs mounted on viewing cards represented one of the most popular photographic commod-ities, taking viewers on three-dimensional arm-chair expeditions.

The relationship also involved the intentions, sentiments, and aesthetics of the men and women behind the camera. Many photographers of the period worked out of commercial studios. In pursuit of appealing representations of the exotic, they sometimes manipulated their im-ages, using professional models, painted back-drops, studio costumes, and contrived poses (figs. 25 and 26). Photographers for government and scientific expeditions, too, varied in their use of manipulation. Native American delega-tions to Washington, D.C., for example, were sometimes posed against painted backdrops and constructed props (fig. 27) or dressed up in the photographer's idea of authentic Indian regalia and settings (Scherer 1973:150–151). John K. Hillers, official photographer of the Bureau of American Ethnology and one of the first profes-sional anthropological photographers, produced remarkable images of southwestern peoples and scenes in the 1870s (fig. 28), some of which come closer to our conception of documentary realism today.

"After breakfast the Maj. [John Wesley Powell], [E. O.] Beaman, Jack [Hillers], [Stephen Van-diver] Jones and Fred [Dellenbaugh] and myself rowed upstream for about a mile in the 'Cañonita.' Landed at a gulch leading up the right wall of the cañon. After a long weary climb of about 1¼ hours up 1200 or 1300 feet and walking along a smooth plateau of white sandstone, we got a view of a country that repaid us of old for all our hard work in lugging these 'mountain howitzers,' the dark tent and camera boxes up."

Journal of Walter Clement Powell
Second Powell Colorado River Expedition
16 September 1871

21
John K. Hillers, ca. 1880
Albumen print
Santo Domingo Pueblo, Rio Grande valley,
New Mexico

Hillers was one of the photographers of the Powell surveys and the first official photographer of the Bureau of American Ethnology and the United States Geological Survey. His photograph of the Keresan pueblo of Santo Domingo, made from a glass-plate negative, shows his photographic equipment wagon and portable processing tent.

22
Antonio Beato, ca. 1903
Albumen print
Queen Nefretari, Temple of Luxor, Egypt

Beato established a
photographic studio in
Luxor in the 1860s.
His exaggerated cam-
era angle, use of dra-
matic natural light, and

effective composition
enhance the majestic
and romantic qualities
of the ancient Egyptian
queen.

23
Nicholas and Company, Madras, ca. 1860–1880
Albumen print
Yimapoonan Temple, Mahabalipuram, India

A romantic spirit in-
fused British represen-
tations of the Indian
subcontinent, and even
photographs of archae-
ological subjects tended

to be more picturesque
than scientific (cf.
Haworth-Booth
1984:104).

24
Baron von Stillfried studio, ca. 1880s
Hand-colored albumen print
Samurai warrior, Japan

Unlike much nineteenth-century documentation of foreign cultures, images made by Western photographers in Japan show that most of the Japanese maintained their own identity in front of the camera without being shadowed by Western interpretation. The photographers themselves showed a sensitivity to Japanese aesthetics, evident in their beautifully composed scenes, often hand-colored by Japanese artisans in the manner of traditional woodblock prints (Worswick 1979). Baron von Stillfried, an Austrian nobleman, operated a photographic studio in Yokohama, one of the treaty ports open to foreigners.

25
Arnoux, ca. 1860–1880
Albumen print
Dames turques prenant le café
("Turkish ladies taking coffee")

During its early years, photography was perceived as a factual means of communication, a break from artistic subjectivity. But photographers, like painters, had ways of controlling how a subject was presented to the viewer. Employing different techniques, each "painted" an individualized picture of reality. Arnoux, a photographer working out of Port Said, Egypt, presents a romanticized view of life in the Turkish harem, using models, costumes, props, a painted backdrop, and carefully designed composition and lighting. Many of these studio photographs tell us more about Western preconceptions than about ethnic lifeways.

26
Bonfils studio, ca. 1867–1895
Albumen print
Jeune femme turque ("Young Turkish woman")

The commercial photographers of the Middle East sometimes "borrowed" each other's images, putting their own imprints or signatures on others' photographs. Different photographers also used the same studio backdrops and props, making definite identification of the source of some prints difficult. This photograph from an original Bonfils catalogue displays the identical backdrop and fan as the signed Arnoux photograph of "Turkish" women.

27
Charles M. Bell, 1877
Albumen print
Ponca delegation, Washington, D.C.

Painted portraits of the
members of Native
American delegations
to Washington, D.C.,
were done until the
1850s, when studio
photographers includ-
ing Alexander Gardner,
A. Zeno Shindler, and
Bell began to make
photographic likenesses

instead. Painted back-
drops and constructed
props (a papier-mâché
boulder here) simulated
western landscapes.
Some photographers
also kept a supply of
costumes on hand for
their subjects to wear
when photographed.

28
John K. Hillers, 1879–1880
Albumen print
The Governor's house, Zuñi Pueblo, New Mexico

Hillers, like other early
photographs of the
American Indian,
sometimes posed or
costumed his subjects.
But much of his field

photography in the
Southwest, such as this
image of a Zuñi child,
seems to present a
more realistic vision of
Native American life.

These images, whether created for purely anthropological purposes, provided valuable data
for early anthropologists and offer priceless information today. Nineteenth-century anthropological institutions, while acquiring specimens
and artifacts, also collected travel and expedi-
tionary photographs for research and teaching.
Cartes-de-visite of native types (fig. 29), popular tourist commodities, were acquired by researchers such as Harvard natural historian
Louis Agassiz, who collected photographs of human subjects as data for his analysis of racial
types.

It was fortuitous for anthropologists then and
now that nineteenth-century photographers recognized the importance of preserving elements
of human culture that were in danger of being
altered or lost forever. La Maison Bonfils, a
commercial studio operated by the Bonfils
family in Beirut from 1867 to 1895, was repre-
sentative of this sense of mission. In the introduction to his (unpublished) photographically
illustrated Bible, Adrien Bonfils set forth his intentions (Vaczek and Buckland 1981:105):

> *In this century of steam and electricity every
> thing is being transformed ... even places.
> Already in the ancient Plain of Sharon one
> hears the whistle of the locomotive .... The
> immortal road to Damascus, witness to the
> apostle Paul's conversion, has become no
> more than a vulgar railway! ... Before ...
> progress has completely done its destructive
> job, before this present which is still the past
> has forever disappeared, we have tried, so to
> speak, to fix and immobilize it in a series of
> photographic views.*

29
Ricardo Villaalba, ca. 1870
Hand-colored cartes-de-visite
Aymara Indians, La Paz, Bolivia

Cartes-de-visite (prints
mounted on 2½-inch-
by-3-inch cards) be-
came popular in South
America in the early
1860s, and photo-
graphs of people in na-
tive costume were
made for the tourist
trade. These Aymara
images were collected
from the photographer
in La Paz in 1872 by
Charles Rand, who
gave them to Elizabeth
Agassiz, wife of Har-
vard scientist Louis
Agassiz.

Although they indulged in manipulation of some of their images (see fig. 26), the Bonfils family's documentation of the Middle East was unsurpassed in volume, scope, and artistic achievement. Today the body of their photographic work is invaluable to photoarchaeologists for reconstructing details of costume, architecture, antiquities, and daily life that have since disappeared or been altered (fig. 30) (Gavin 1985; Rockett 1983).

Photographers of the last century mastered an unwieldy craft and brought personal vision to their work. But this new form of communication also created unique and problematic relationships. The Rio Grande pueblo of Santo Domingo that John Hillers documented in the 1880s (see fig. 21) was recently photographed from the air during a sacred winter ceremonial, and some of the photographs were published in a local newspaper (*Santa Fe New Mexican* 24 and 29 January 1984). The Santo Domingans, who have prohibited the making of photographs, drawings, and other visual representations on their lands, sued the photographer and the newspaper, thereby exercising their legal and moral right to control the use of the camera within their own community.

The social context of making photographs has altered dramatically in the twentieth century, with issues of consent and self-determination increasingly brought to the fore. These issues have a bearing on the entire anthropological enterprise. While our desire for information recorded and conveyed through the camera persists, we must ask ourselves what influence the photographic image has on its viewers and what consequence it harbors for its subjects. The nineteenth-century record offers insights into the origins of this as yet unresolved relationship between the observer and observed.

30
Bonfils studio, ca. 1867–1895
Albumen print
Arch of Triumph in the ancient caravan city of Palmyra, Syria

Felix Bonfils established his photographic studio in Beirut in 1867. His wife, Lydie, and their son, Adrien, later joined him in the business. After his death, Lydie established studios in Jerusalem and Baalbek and ran the family business until 1916. Abraham Guiragossian then took over the Bonfils name and business and sold platinum prints from Bonfils negatives until at least 1932. Today the Semitic Museum at Harvard University, which houses a large collection of Bonfils photographs, has embarked on an ambitious project of returning copies of these images to their places of origin, where they can be studied locally by historians and anthropologists.

31
Photographer unknown, 1896
Gelatin dry-plate negative
Penobscot women weaving baskets
Indian Island, Old Town, Maine

32
Hillel Burger, 1984
Color transparency
Chitimacha basket, ca. 1900, Louisiana

In the field, time relentlessly marches on, bringing change to all things. Each fleeting glimpse the camera captures of an object *in situ* later provides useful evidence of its history—where it was discovered, how it was created, by whom it was used (fig. 31). Taken out of its original environment, the object is no longer bound by the same constraints of time and place. The museum photographer may create new realizations of it by exploiting the studio setting, exploring the options of the technology, and drawing upon personal vision to extend our powers of observation. The studio setting frees the photographer to direct the camera's focus away from the object's native context and onto the study of its physical content—characteristics of form, size, surface, depth, texture, color, and detail. By isolating an object, the photographer in a sense abstracts it. The abstraction may disorient us, but in the process we are made aware of qualities not appreciated at first sight.

Studying the museum piece, the photographer must come to know its characteristics and meaning. "I strive to bring out the aesthetic qualities of an object by trying to understand the intentions of its maker or what meaning the object had for its users," explains Hillel Burger, staff photographer of the Peabody Museum. The photographer works in cooperation with the museum curator to decide what elements of an object to highlight and communicate to a specific audience. Mediating between anthropologist and audience, the photographer then determines how best to represent the piece.

The museum photographer uses large-format technical cameras that can capture detail, achieve maximum depth of field, and control perspective. Enlargement, lighting, and color are used to create a representation of a North American Chitimacha basket (fig. 32) so vibrant

**33
Hillel Burger, 1985
Black-and-white negative
Shoshonean (probably Mono) storage basket,
ca. 1900, California**

and detailed that we can almost feel its texture. In contrast, minimizing color and photographing from an oblique angle bring out the form and depth of a Shoshonean storage basket (fig. 33). In some instances the studio photographer may have to choose between emphasizing form and revealing detail; accentuating one may result in loss of the other.

One shot cannot always do justice to a very complicated piece. Multiple views can influence the way a viewer perceives an object, opening up new ways of appreciating it, as is demonstrated by these four distinct perspectives of a carved wooden "staff god" from the Cook Islands (figs. 34–37). Strong lighting from one side of the piece brings out its overall form and rhythm (fig. 34), while flat reflected light from the opposite side emphasizes detail (fig. 35). The head-on view (fig. 36) loses some detail but reveals a totally new perspective of the carving's overall form. A two-thirds view suggests the object's roundness and depth (fig. 37).

34 — 37
Hillel Burger, 1980
Black-and-white negatives
Carved wooden image ("staff god"),
before A.D. 1849, Rarotonga, Cook Islands,
Central Polynesia

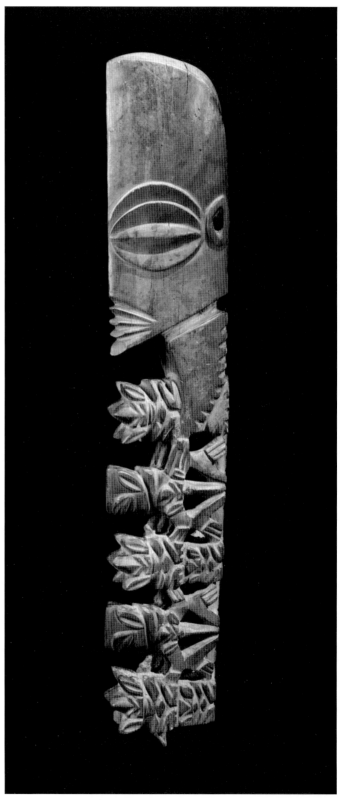

34

35

36

37

Different lighting techniques are used to bring out the fine and shallow details of an object. Indirect lighting contributes to a comprehensive treatment of the incised markings on a cuneiform tablet from Iraq (fig. 38). The background is minimized, and the tablet itself occupies most of the image area. The mythological animal on the tablet is examined and emphasized in a closeup view (fig. 39) with the help of special lighting effects (including low-angle and multidirectional light).

Sometimes drawings and photographic images can successfully complement each other. The photograph and drawing of a Caddoan pot from the Lower Mississippi valley together bring out the form of the ceramic as well as its detailed incisions and marks of manufacture (fig. 40). With the passage of time these incisions had become very shallow; they needed better clarification than the camera could achieve. While the photograph recreates the exact shape of the object, the drawing clearly presents its decorative detail.

38
Hillel Burger, 1985
Black-and-white negative
Clay tablet with incised cuneiform writing,
ca. 1500 B.C., Iraq

39
Hillel Burger, 1985
Black-and-white negative
Detail of cuneiform tablet

40
Hillel Burger, 1979
Black-and-white negative
Caddoan (Natchitoches Engraved) bottle,
ca. mid-1700s, Ouachita region, north-central
Louisiana

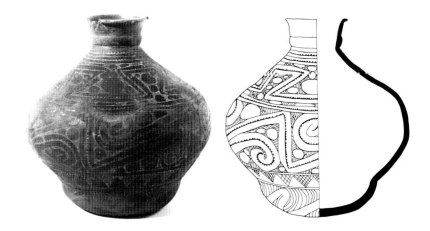

The use of background and lighting in color photography helps to create the mood of a final image. A light background, for example, reveals the soft quality of the surface of a gold mask from the Coclé ceremonial site of Sitio Conte in Panama (fig. 41). In figure 42, its softness is still apparent, but a grey background provides a more balanced contrast to the gold. The dramatic black background in figure 43 creates good separation, stressing the overall shape and color of the piece; direct lighting emphasizes the precise delineation of the pattern and the object's symmetry. The use of multidirectional lights (with blue and red reflections) overglamorizes, accentuating the shining precious metal (fig. 44) and underplaying other, less striking qualities of the object.

Objects and (later) photographs acquired or taken in the field as a result of nineteenth-century exploration were deposited in museums and research institutes. As anthropology emerged as a professional endeavor, these institutions also sent out their own expeditions to gather extensive collections for research. Before the invention of photography, illustrators were employed to present visually collections and accounts of field research. Photography later served this purpose and was used additionally as a means of documenting collections for record-keeping purposes. Today the photographer's images of museum objects and copies of historical photographs serve as a source of illustration for museum catalogues, textbooks, periodicals, scholarly publications, exhibitions, and audiovisual presentations. The photograph, journeying where the object cannot go, reaches a worldwide community that depends on the image for its understanding of anthropological materials. Hillel Burger acknowledges the responsibility entailed in conveying messages about cultural objects: "One must always balance the power of the medium with a degree of modesty and austerity."

41

42

41–44
Hillel Burger, 1985
Color transparencies
Gold mask from Sitio Conte, ca. A.D. 500
Coclé Province, Panama

43

44

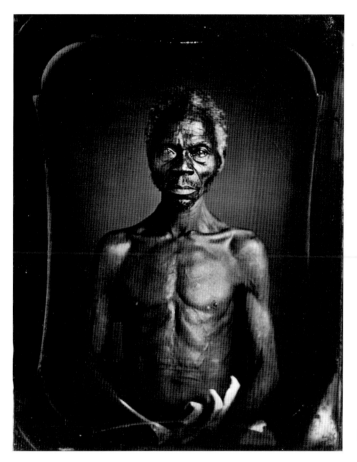

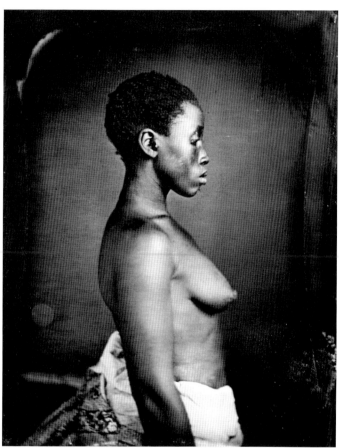

45
J. T. Zealy, 1850
Daguerreotype
Renty, an African-born slave, South Carolina

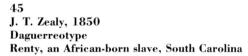

46
J. T. Zealy, 1850
Daguerreotype
Delia, daughter of Renty, South Carolina

Renty and Delia were slaves on a South Carolina plantation when these daguerreotypes were taken in 1850. Commissioned by Louis Agassiz to provide data for his racial theories, the fifteen front, side, **and back views now in the Peabody Museum's Photographic Archives are rare images of American slavery and graphic reminders that not all studio photography in the nineteenth century was voluntary.**

5

Biological Anthropology: Evolution from Daguerreotype to Satellite

Photographing ... may have to be done by the roadside, in the field, or under other untoward circumstances which will often call for the exercise of not a little ingenuity. [The anthropologist] may at first be received with suspicion and suffer for the faults of others. But with a fair interpreter, friendly, honest attitude, and such small gifts as may best be fitted to the occasion, the student will as a rule secure the needed observations.

Aleš Hrdlička, 1920
Anthropometry

Nineteenth-century biological anthropology, the study of people as biological organisms, was concerned primarily with body measurements and classification of human racial types. Like most science of the period, it was conducted on the human scale, within what Philip and Phylis Morrison in *Powers of Ten* (1982) have called the "domain of familiarity." Direct observation of skulls, skeletons, and body types was relied on during this early period for research data, illustration of theory, and evidence for drawing conclusions. In the twentieth century, biological anthropology has subdivided into primatology, hominoid evolution studies, genetics, human variation studies, and other specialized fields. In all of them, photography has expanded its critical role in research, teaching, and publicity. As instruments of modern science have extended our vision into entirely new domains of scale, biological anthropologists have moved far beyond knowledge accessible by direct visual perception to knowledge available only from instrument and inference. Generally speaking, this has meant a shift from an interest in external characteristics to the study of internal structures, their functions, and evolution. The photograph has followed a related path of development from daguerreotype to X-ray to satellite image.

Problems of Power and Consent: Racial and Ethnic Typologies

The year 1839, in which Daguerre's new photographic process was announced to the public, coincidentally marked the beginnings of biological anthropology as a recognized scientific field in the United States. In *Crania Americana*, Samuel George Morton, a Philadelphia physician, challenged the Biblical account of creation with the theory of polygenesis, which held that distinct human races, or types, had been created separately in the different regions of the earth to which they were specifically suited. Although riddled with statistical errors and unconscious bias, Morton's craniometry, along with his later publication, *Crania Aegyptiaca* (1844), appeared to some members of the scientific community to provide empirical proof of the separate creation and persistent inferiority of Native Americans and Black Africans (Gould 1981:30–72).

Louis Agassiz, the natural historian who founded Harvard University's Museum of Comparative Zoology, considered Morton's work a central support for his own theory that all species, including humans, had been divinely created for certain "zoological provinces" (Stanton 1960:100–112). To confirm the existence of biologically distinct human groups and to test for the persistence of racial characteristics through time and environmental change, Agassiz sought reliable visual evidence of anatomical variation among African-born slaves and their American-born progeny in the pre–Civil War United States. He accordingly studied, measured, and had photographed at least eight individuals from different tribes and regions of Africa (including two of their American-born offspring), all of whom were working on plantations outside of Columbia, South Carolina (figs. 45 and 46). The fifteen daguerreotypes that he commissioned from photographer J. T. Zealy are unprecedented early examples of the scientific use of photography as well as extremely rare images of African Americans before the Civil War.

These images raise disturbing questions about the anthropological camera as a weapon of power, a problem inherent in the ambiguous relationship between photographer and subject, as noted by Susan Sontag (1977), Roland Barthes (1981), and others. Because the relationship between photographer and living human subject is far more problematic cross-culturally than within a single culture, the terms and results of the anthropological photographic encounter must be carefully assessed. While studio portraits were an index of social success for the prospering middle classes of industrialized societies, the Zealy daguerreotypes were undertaken in a context of dominance and oppression. Their subjects presumably had little to say about the ways in which they were visually presented.

Agassiz assembled a large collection of photographs of human subjects, including cartes-de-visite (see fig. 29) and albums of racial types (see fig. 48). During a zoological expedition to Brazil in 1865, Agassiz and his student, Walter Hunnewell, photographed male and female Indians, Blacks, and mixed racial types in the standard front, back, and profile views of natural history specimens (fig. 47). Each sitter was viewed first fully clothed, then (in many cases) clothed only from the waist down, and finally fully disrobed. Elizabeth C. Agassiz's comments (Agassiz and Agassiz 1868:276–277) on her husband's research reveal the reluctance of the subjects:

> *The grand difficulty is found in the prejudices of the people themselves. There is a prevalent superstition among the Indians and Negroes that a portrait absorbs into itself something of the vitality of the sitter, and that any one is liable to die shortly after his picture is taken. This notion is so deeply rooted that it has been no easy matter to overcome it. However, of late the desire to see themselves in a picture is gradually gaining the ascendant, the example of a few courageous ones having emboldened the more timid, and models are much more easily obtained than they were at first.*

Between the lines of this passage one can see the photographer-researcher as an agent of cultural disruption and change, presenting the native population with unprecedented choices. The Brazilians were unaware of the purposes of the photographs, but unlike the subjects of the Zealy daguerreotypes they had in a certain sense consented. According to the Agassiz account, some models began to pose voluntarily, risking a perceived danger in order to see themselves in a photograph.

The anthropologist cannot completely control the photograph or its interpretations and subsequent uses—any more than we can in reproducing these images here. We trust that their historical significance, along with the passage of time, mitigates any possible offense. As in the Zealy portraits, "the vitality of the sitter" is indeed captured, transcending the intentions of either Agassiz or his photographer. As Elinor Reichlin, who originally identified the daguerreotypes, noted (1977:5),

> *it is ironic that these pictures, made to demonstrate the supposed inferiority of their subjects, instead conferred a kind of immortality on the men and women we know only as Renty and Delia, Jem and Jack. It was no consolation for the humiliation they endured both as slaves and as objects of scientific curiosity, but a rare gain for those who now encounter these people as memorably real survivors of a painful epoch.*

In 1850 the camera had already become a useful and probing tool, with both the potential for abuse and the ability to record for posterity some essential truths about the human condition.

There was intense debate in the United States during the 1850s and 1860s over competing theories of creation and evolution, with views such as Agassiz's used in support of the institution of slavery. The Peabody Museum was founded by George Peabody in the midst of this controversy. He instructed the trustees to address "the great questions as to the order of development of the animal kingdom and of the

"Still, there is something predatory in the act of taking a picture. To photograph people is to violate them by seeing them as they never see themselves, by having knowledge of them they can never have; it turns people into objects that can be symbolically possessed."

Susan Sontag, 1977
On Photography

47
Walter Hunnewell and Louis Agassiz, 1865
Albumen prints
Four prints of a Brazilian woman, Manaus, Brazil

It is not always clear when consent has been given to photograph an individual or a community. In her journal of the 1865 Brazilian expedition, Elizabeth C. Agassiz (Agassiz and Agassiz 1868) recorded the initial reluctance and eventual aquiescence of Agassiz's and Hunnewell's subjects, pointing out the role of conflicting beliefs and unequal power relationships in the photographic encounter.

"With no words to guide us, we are as free as we wish to conjure up identifications or contexts, creating the meaning from what we bring to the image."

Ira Jacknis, 1984
"Franz Boas and Photography"

48
Photographer unknown, ca. 1860s
Albumen print
Andaman Islanders, Bay of Bengal, India

These Andaman Islanders pose with a Mr. Honfray, whose height (5 feet 5 inches) serves as an indication of theirs. Presented to the Anthropological Society of Paris by a former governor of the Andaman Islands, the photograph appeared in a volume of racial types entitled "Negroes and Sundries," part of a set produced by the Museum of Paris (now the Musée de l'Homme). Lack of ethnographic documentation makes such photographs particularly intriguing and frustrating. The image could portray a single family or a group of unrelated individuals. Note the chain of physical contact and the studied gaze of the European, directed away from the group: a composition that could result from the photographer's technical improvisations (perhaps a means of keeping the subjects stationary for the long exposure) or could indicate a deeper, cultural significance.

human race, which have lately been so much discussed" (Peabody Museum 1866:1). But the subject was still a painful one in the decades following the Civil War, and biological anthropology in the United States suffered a period of relative decline and disinterest.

Outside the United States strong traditions of research continued. In France, Paul Broca, Paul Topinard, and the Anthropological Society of Paris engaged in classifying the shapes and sizes of human types, especially those in the extensive French colonial empire. The photographer for the Anthropological Society of Paris, L. Rousseau, photographed scores of foreign visitors to the capital city in the 1850s and 1860s, and original prints of these portraits, along with others collected from various sources, were gathered in ornate photographic albums. Sold by subscription, they found homes in scientific institutions and the libraries of the wealthy. One six-volume set, believed to have been acquired by Louis Agassiz, is now in Harvard's Tozzer Library (fig. 48). The photographs in these compilations of racial and ethnic types were generally assembled without regard to ethnographic context, which was not considered pertinent to a study of racial physiology. Today's researchers are often tantalized and frustrated by this lack of documentation, which increases the difficulty of eliciting meaning from photographic images.

Anthropology at the Fair

With the appearance of anthropology at museums and expositions in the late nineteenth century, biological anthropology began to reach a broader public. At the World's Columbian Exposition held in Chicago in 1893, Frederic Ward Putnam, director of the Peabody Museum, and Franz Boas, a seminal figure in the development of American anthropology, set up a Laboratory of Physical Anthropology. One wall of the laboratory was covered with photographs of human physical types to which visitors could compare themselves (Johnson 1898: 327, 349). The laboratory was among the popular attractions at the Exposition, and visitors

were invited to participate as subjects of anthropological research. Putnam and Boas had serious scientific intentions, but they discovered that public anthropology ran the risk of pandering to existing vanities and prejudices. The ideological intent of such expositions encouraged visitors to celebrate their industrial civilization, which they tended to see as proof of their racial superiority (Rydell 1984). Rather than teaching a tolerance for human differences, measuring individuals at a charge of fifty cents a head and comparing physical appearances by means of photographs may have invited self-centered bias.

The World's Columbian Exposition also gave rise to coffee-table photograph albums of the "races of mankind" such as *Portrait Types of the Midway Plaisance* (fig. 49) (Chicago 1894). "All the world is here!" was the motto of the Midway, the amusement section of the fair, where native villages populated with authentic ethnic "types" were found alongside restaurants and carnival attractions. As he indicated in his introduction to *Portrait Types*, Putnam saw it as an object lesson in 1890s-style cosmopolitanism. He thought that its famous "Street in Cairo" made visitors question the very definition of dance, since "every nation had its own form" (ibid.). From atop the Ferris Wheel—a technological wonder introduced at the Exposition— one could "view this mimic world as from another planet," he enthused, and "look down upon an enchanted land filled with happy folk. Truly there was much of instruction as well as of joy on the Merry Midway" (ibid.).

Or so Putnam hoped. His humanist vision was not entirely realized even in the descriptions accompanying the "portrait types" (figs. 50 and 51). Intended to promote cross-cultural respect, these materials were in all probability consumed by the public as sources of amused curiosity. Accordingly, the anthropology that visitors took home from the fair generally confirmed rather than challenged their preconceptions (Rydell 1984).

49
World's Columbian Exposition, 1894
Cover, *Portrait Types of the Midway Plaisance*

"All the world is here!" Frederic Ward Putnam, in his attempt to foster cosmopolitanism and cross-cultural understanding at the Exposition, wrote that the anthropological exhibits "almost make one wish he might live in a country where life is so easy and where tailors' and dressmakers' bills are unknown trials" (Chicago 1894). Despite the spirit of good-natured tolerance that infused *Portrait Types*, the photographic album and its captions failed to avoid ethnic stereotypes of the time.

50
Place and Coover, 1893
Portrait Types of the Midway Plaisance, 1894
"Mary Dookshoode Annanuck (Eskimo)"

"The Eskimo [Inuit] are the widest spread aboriginal people in the world, occupying the whole Arctic coast of America and a small portion of the Asiatic shore of Behring Strait, thus stretching a distance of three thousand two hundred miles. They are short in stature and their skin is of so light a brown that, when clean, red shows in the cheeks of children and young women. In summer they live in conical skin tents and in winter, at times in snow houses, but usually in half-underground huts built of stone, earth and bones, and entered on all fours by a long tunnel-like passage. They live by hunting and fishing and are enormous eaters. In intelligence they rank well among barbarous races, have considerable humor and are notable mimics. Their language is peculiar; they have an extensive folk-lore and some published literature.... This woman ...is a vigorous type of the race..." (Chicago 1894).

"Truly there was much of instruction as well as of joy on the Merry Midway."

Frederic Ward Putnam, 1894
Portrait Types of the Midway Plaisance

51
Place and Coover, 1893
Portrait Types of the Midway Plaisance, 1894
"Mr. E. Ruscheweyh (Leader of the German Infantry Band)"

"This gentleman, Mr. Ruscheweyh, was chosen as leader of the infantry band of forty-eight pieces that furnished music at the German Village and elsewhere. He is a typical German soldier and a veteran of three great wars. This number of the Types of the Midway contains portraits which are, generally speaking, of a more highly intellectual character than any that have preceded; nearly all of the subjects being men of eminence and social position in their respective countries. It is, in fact, the 'civilized' portfolio of the work" (Chicago 1894).

The Hooton Era: Measurements and Judgments

After 1900 biological anthropology began to gain new academic respectability in the United States. Earnest A. Hooton at Harvard University's Anthropology Department and Aleš Hrdlička at the Smithsonian Institution's U.S. National Museum dominated and directed American biological anthropology in the first half of the twentieth century. Hrdlička established a journal and a professional society, while Hooton taught a generation of followers. Successors to both Morton and Broca, Hrdlička and Hooton evinced strong strains of romantic racism and biological determinism. Hooton clearly saw what he considered a positive social application to his racial analysis.

Hooton took advantage of laboratory photography, supplementing traditional anatomical measurements with visual documentation of body types, or "somatotypes" (cf. Sheldon 1942, 1954). His various projects for the U.S. Army, for example, were based on thousands of photographs. In a 1946 study more than one hundred thousand men were measured and nearly fifty thousand photographed in order to classify body build types (Hooton 1951). From these Army studies to his intergenerational study of Harvard fathers and sons (Hooton and Stagg 1953), Hooton relied heavily on photographs of somatotypes for analysis and teaching.

Hooton believed that photographs—purely visual evidence—could reveal important truths about the laws of human physical variation. In his 1930 study of skeletal remains of the Indians of Pecos, New Mexico, he prepared composite photographs of what he considered distinct morphological types, then demonstrated their distinctness by comparing them with other types, even making composites of composites (fig. 52). Peabody Museum ethnologist Alice C. Fletcher had used the technique earlier (see fig. 96), but Hooton's approach contrasts sharply with her cautious but sympathetic conclusions. Hooton used his composites as a "final test of the reality of these type subgroups" (Hooton 1930:227), which he had formulated through a visual and statistical comparison of the Pecos

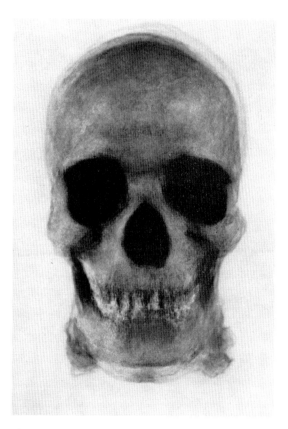

52
Earnest A. Hooton, 1930
Composite photograph
Composite of all composite skull types,
Pecos Pueblo, New Mexico

Composite photographs combine two or more images to make a single photograph. As part of his study of the skeletal remains of the Indians of Pecos Pueblo, Hooton prepared composite photographs of what he considered distinct morphological cranial types in order to get a general picture of each. Ten skulls of each type were carefully aligned and exposed on a single plate. He then compared the types to each other by making composites of these composites. The composite of all composites was "very fuzzy" (Hooton 1930:230), but Hooton felt that it represented his overall impression of the skulls in the Pecos series. Although hardly meeting the requirements of scientific evidence, this method was considered by Hooton valid, if laborious.

"We must either do some biological housecleaning or delude ourselves with the futile hope that a government of the unfit, for the unfit, and by the unfit will not perish from the earth."

Earnest A. Hooton
"What Shall We Do To Be Saved?"
Harvard Alumni Bulletin, **5 March 1937**

skulls with what he termed three "advanced" (Plains, European, and Alpine) and three "primitive" (Basket Maker, Negroid, and Australoid) racial types. "On the whole I feel that the method of photograph composites offers a great deal of value in the analysis of a cranial population," he concluded (ibid.:230). It had, he asserted, "furnished the ultimate proof of the validity of our morphological types" (ibid.). Rather than any "ultimate proof," he had discovered the seductive capacity of the photographic image, in this case its ability to create a convincing "reality" to illustrate his morphological determinations.

Hooton brought biological anthropology to wide public attention and was featured frequently in the popular press (fig. 53) (Stockly 1939). He illustrated his theories of criminality—in which he attributed certain crimes to racial predispositions—and his observations on human evolution with cartoons, suggestive photographs, and irreverent titles: *Apes, Men, and Morons* (1937a), *Why Men Behave Like Apes and Vice Versa* (1940), and *Man's Poor Relations* (1942). If his hypotheses of human variation and race have fallen into disrepute, Hooton's appreciation of photography for study, teaching, and publicity has not. This is particularly apparent today in the fields of primatology and hominoid evolution.

53
Arthur Griffin, 1939
Life magazine, **7 August 1939**

Hooton popularized biological anthropology in the United States during the period between the world wars, an era of growing public interest in race and eugenics. *Life* reported that "Professor Hooton, not content to measure bones and chart faces...has put anthropology on the front pages. From his study of the history of man as an animal, Hooton offers an answer to the question of why our social engine has stalled. 'Maybe,' he suggests, 'somebody has watered the gasoline'" (Stockly 1939).

"At the time I took these photographs, none of us had any idea how complex primate behavior would prove to be."

Irven DeVore, 1985

"A High Order of Social Negotiation": Primatology in Africa

Partly in reaction against Hooton's descriptive racial typology, his student Sherwood Washburn and a few other researchers began after World War II to examine relationships between anatomical change, locomotor adaptations, and primate social behavior. These new directions in functional anatomy—watching behavior as well as describing structure—have aimed toward a consistent theory of human and nonhuman primate evolution (Washburn 1977; Ribnick 1982:59).

The pioneering work on baboons in the wild by Harvard's Irven DeVore, which began in 1959 (DeVore 1963, 1965), demonstrates ways in which still and motion picture photography serve as central tools in biological anthropology research. In order to study primate behavior DeVore records photographic sequences, either series of still photographs or segments of motion picture footage documenting activities or interactions. Behavior as an object of study cannot be served by single still photographs alone; the sequence of actions through time can increase analytic significance. Improvements in photographic technology over the last thirty years have greatly enhanced the ability of primatologists to observe and interpret behavior. The telephoto lens permits nonintrusive, long-distance recording, and the development of 400-foot, easy-loading film reels allows one to record extended behavioral sequences without interruption. In the 1960s the introduction of fast, fine-grained, high-resolution films yielded much sharper detail in field images. Using photography to record behavior has an additional advantage: it enables the anthropologist to "bring the field back home" to the laboratory or classroom. Students are now trained in observation methods by reviewing film loops or photo sequences from the field.

Primatologists have amassed a significant corpus of photographic records, reanalysis of which

54a
Irven DeVore, 1959
Black-and-white print from a color transparency
A dominant adult male baboon bites an infant as a subordinate male watches.
Nairobi National Park, Kenya

Photographic sequences provide important visual evidence of primate behavior for immediate study as well as future reanalysis. DeVore interpreted this sequence, shot over twenty years ago, as a dominant adult male baboon "disciplining" an infant while another adult male looked on. With increased understanding of baboon social behavior, reexamination yields a new interpretation (cf. Smuts 1985). "By attacking the infant, the more dominant male is asserting himself over the other adult male— the infant's friend— without risking injury in a fight with the male himself." (DeVore 1985: personal communication).

54b
Irven DeVore, 1959
Black-and-white print from a color transparency
Infant baboon cowers on the ground.

has begun to yield new interpretations. The sequence shown in figure 54, for example, which DeVore shot in 1959, was initially interpreted as a dominant male baboon disciplining an infant while another male baboon watched (Eimerl and DeVore 1965:124–125). Restudy of the same behavior by Barbara Smuts (1985) suggests that we may be seeing much more complicated social relationships than was originally realized. The more dominant male may, in fact, be biting the infant to warn the less dominant male, who stands awkwardly and ambivalently at a distance. This behavior appears to be part of a larger pattern of male relationships not yet fully understood, "but in part the infant is a hapless pawn in an aggressive episode between the two adult males" (DeVore 1985: personal communication). "At the time I took these photographs," DeVore notes, "none of us had any idea how complex primate behavior would prove to be" (ibid.). The reexamined images now portray to primatologists "a rather high order of complex social negotiation" (ibid.), information not perceived twenty years ago.

Pondering the Skull of *Sivapithecus*

What must prehumans have been like? To answer this question biological anthropologists have followed many paths. While primatologists continue to observe primate behavior in the wild and in the laboratory, paleoanthropologists, broadening the search for human origins and evolution in Europe, Africa, and Asia, are emerging with a complex picture of development that extends over some twenty million years.

Paleoanthropologists have amplified and intensified their field data through the use of macrophotography, microphotography, and instant photography. During the 1979–1980 field season, a new hominoid skull—that of the eight-million-year-old Asian ape *Sivapithecus indicus*—was discovered by a joint Yale University/Geological Survey of Pakistan expedition under the direction of paleoanthropologist David Pilbeam, now at Harvard (Pilbeam 1982). Excavation of the skull was accompanied at all times

54c
Irven DeVore, 1959
Black-and-white print from a color transparency
Adult baboon walks away as screaming infant
begins to rise.

"If we want to understand the evolutionary history of any group, . . . we need a 'branching sequence' (the order in which species split off), dates for the branching events, some notion of what possible ancestors looked like, some ideas about their important adaptations, and knowledge about their environments and environmental change. . . . Our challenge now is to understand ...how to look at the anatomy with fresh eyes in order to see underlying similarities."

David Pilbeam, 1983
"Hominoid evolution"

by the camera. Conventional photographic media such as 35mm color slides (fig. 55) were used to record each stage of discovery and excavation. Instant photographs provided immediate annotation in the field. Attached to site cards, they document site locations by recording geographical landmarks and other visual cues that enhance the written records of maps and field notes (fig. 56).

The geographical setting of the *Sivapithecus* site, the Potwar Plateau region of Pakistan, is examined in much broader terms by means of Landsat satellite photographs (fig. 57). This

space-eye view places the home of the ancient ape in its current geological and stratigraphic context. In the museum laboratory, the skeletal material of *Sivapithecus* is subjected to a series of photographic analyses, including scanning electron microscopy, X-ray photography, and CAT (computer-assisted tomography) scan, all of which yield specific data about the unusually complete skull fragment. Electron microscopy of the teeth, for instance, has revealed considerable wear, indicating that the food of *Sivapithecus* was mainly vegetal and often tough (Pilbeam 1983:15). X-ray photographs permit

55
Kay Behrensmeyer, 1979
Black-and-white print from a color transparency
Excavation of skull of *Sivapithecus indicus*,
Pakistan

During excavation the archaeological site is in a state of continual alteration. Anthropologists employ the camera to preserve visually each stage of the process.

56
Mark Solomon, 1979
Instant black-and-white print
Site card documenting location of discovery of
Sivapithecus indicus

The great advantage of instant images is, of course, their immediacy: there is no question that the required material has been successfully recorded, no waiting for results. While still at the site, anthropologists can make annotations on the print itself, marking the exact location of the fossil discovery and other relevant information.

57
Earth Resources Orbiting Satellite, 1981
Satellite photograph
Potwar Plateau region, Pakistan

Satellite images are made from orbiting satellites with scanners that record the earth's image in binary code. Records are made in various wavelengths and then radio transmitted to an earth receiving station where a computer processes the information. For paleoanthropologists studying the remains of *Sivapithecus indicus*, satellite images show precisely how fossil sites are related to local geological features. They also provide information important in helping to select new areas for survey and excavation.

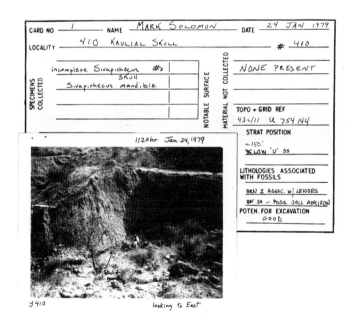

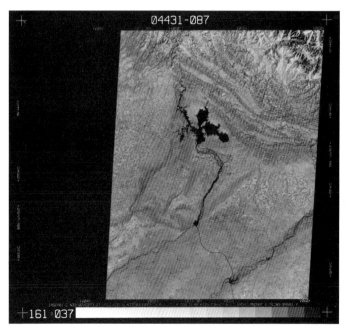

comparison of external features with those of
other primates. The CAT scan (fig. 58) brings
out three-dimensional internal features, the architecture of the skull, by taking visual cross
sections or "slices" of the bone. This procedure
is particularly valuable where dense bone is encountered, providing new information about the
anatomy and, by inference, the behavior patterns of *Sivapithecus*.

As is the case with so much of modern science,
paleoanthropology has highly technical and specialized aspects, but the search for human
ancestors has never enjoyed more general popularity than it does today. This is so, in part,
because the photograph has brought the search
back home, serving as a bridge to understanding. According to Pilbeam (1983:15), *Sivapithecus* is "the best known hominoid from anywhere
between three and twenty million years old."
Eight million years after his death, he stares
out from the cover of *Nature* magazine as a hol-
low-eyed mirror for humanity (fig. 59). Like
Renty and Delia, he stimulates our curiosity
and invites our inquiry into the meaning of the
human past and the prospects of a seemingly
precarious human future.

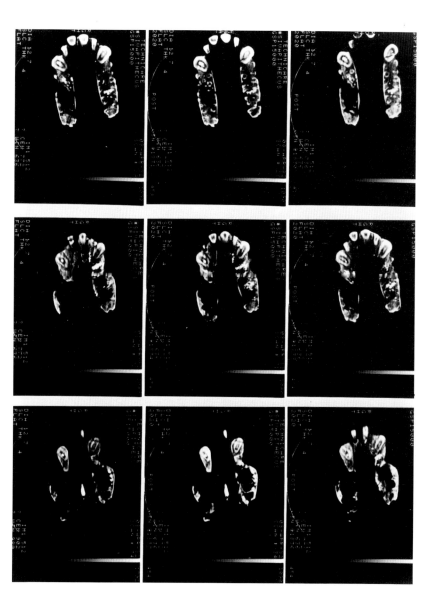

58
**Steven Ward, Glenn Conroy, and Michael Vannier,
1985**
Computer-assisted tomography (CAT scan)
Skull of *Sivapithecus indicus*

A CAT scan image, like
an X-ray image, uses
high-energy radiation
of extremely short
wavelengths to pene-
trate and reveal the in-
ternal structure of an
object placed between
the radiation source
and the recording film.
The resulting image re-
flects the degree of ab-
sorption and density of
the material and pro-
duces visual cross sec-
tions of the object's
internal structure. Pro-
viding information
about the anatomy of
Sivapithecus, CAT
scans enabled research-
ers to create a com-
plete graphic
reconstruction of the
skull from the fossil
fragment.

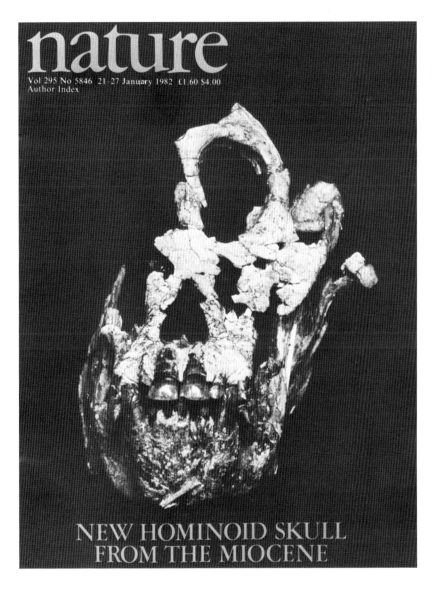

nature

Vol 295 No 5846 21–27 January 1982 £1.60 $4.00
Author Index

NEW HOMINOID SKULL
FROM THE MIOCENE

59
William Sacco, 1982
Cover, *Nature*, 21–27 January 1982
Sivapithecus indicus

Photography plays a vital role in bringing anthropology to the public's attention, which, in turn, can generate support for scientific research.

Prominent exposure of this "portrait" of *Sivapithecus* serves both public and professional interests.

60
W. Simpson, 1877
Cover, *Illustrated London News*, 3 February 1877
Artist Simpson sketching the acropolis at
Mycenae, site of Schliemann's excavations

Before photolitho-
graphic processes were
perfected, illustrated
newspapers relied on
artists' renderings of
news and feature sto-
ries. Some were done
on location, others
were copied from pho-
tographs taken in the
field. The *Illustrated*

London News avidly
followed Heinrich
Schliemann's excava-
tions in the eastern
Mediterranean in the
1870s, simultaneously
responding to and stim-
ulating its readers' hun-
ger for pictorial and
verbal accounts of ar-
chaeological adventure.

THE ILLUSTRATED LONDON NEWS.

REGISTERED AT THE GENERAL POST-OFFICE FOR TRANSMISSION ABROAD.

No. 1960.—VOL. LXX.   SATURDAY, FEBRUARY 3, 1877.   WITH TWO SUPPLEMENTS | SIXPENCE. By Post, 6½d.

ANTIQUARIAN DISCOVERIES IN GREECE: OUR ARTIST SKETCHING THE ENTRANCE GATE OF THE ACROPOLIS AT MYCENÆ.

6

Archaeology: Intermingling of Human Past and Present through the Camera's Eye

To copy the millions of hieroglyphics which cover even the exterior of the great monuments of Thebes, Memphis, Karnak, and others would require decades of time and legions of draughts-men. By daguerreotype one person would suffice to accomplish this immense work successfully.... These designs will excel the works of the most accomplished painters, in fidelity of detail and true reproduction of the local atmosphere.

Dominique François Jean Arago, 1839

Photography was enthusiastically received by archaeologists from its first introduction. Applied in the field as a labor-saving device, it functions later as a spur to memory and a store-house of data. Living in a civilization that increasingly communicates in visual and symbolic terms—a "hieroglyphic civilization," as cultural historian Warren Susman (1984) has called it—archaeologists discovered early the value of communicating visually to the public and the profession. As a consequence, few scientific fields have used photography as variously and experimentally as archaeology, and few have enjoyed such public enthusiasm mediated by this technology. Drawing on the photographic record of their predecessors, archaeologists may revisit a familiar site, explore similar ones, and build cumulative knowledge in an inquiry that extends across generations. Often the public watches the process, looking directly over professional shoulders and into the trenches. And archaeologists make appeal, in words and pictures, for public support and approval (Fagan 1984). One result of this dialectic has been a large body of visual material that captures the intermingling of human past and present.

Archaeology has always been the most open, professionally porous branch of anthropology, partly because of the inherent general appeal of materials from the human past and partly because of accessibility to the field, which could be a backyard as easily as an Egyptian tomb. As a discipline it has been fractious, unwieldy,

and difficult to contain, with many epicenters of authority and loyalty even within separate national traditions. At the same time, its openness has encouraged an unusual degree of experimentation and borrowing of concepts, methods, and tools from widespread sources. The incorporation of specializations like paleobotany, geology, climatology, paleoecology, and archaeometallurgy—along with sophisticated photographic technologies—exemplifies this characteristic.

The interaction between technology and theory has been complex, developing unevenly as a function of the capabilities of photographic technologies and/or changes in archaeological thinking. Aerial archaeology, for example, while conceivable in the 1860s and certainly feasible by 1910, awaited impetus from military and commercial interests between 1920 and 1940. This was partly due to the logistical difficulties of managing bulky equipment, but the deeper explanation lies in the fact that archaeologists, engrossed in specific sites and their artifacts, had developed little regional vision. Aerial photography helped to develop such vision but was also dependent on an intellectual climate receptive to its potential. In other cases, technological limitations have been more clearly determinative. Artifact analysis and typology in the last century was largely morphological and taxonomic, chiefly because these studies developed out of the natural history of the period, with its fascination with external forms and presumption that form indicates function. But emphasis on external form also resulted from the fact that techniques of microphotography and X-ray photography that permit internal structural analysis did not exist. When they appeared, archaeologists found ways to adapt them for their own uses, and theory began to catch up with technology.

Classical Models

To the emerging literate publics of mid-nineteenth-century Western Europe and the United States, hungry for accounts of heroic adventures and pictures of excavated treasures from the past, archaeology was endlessly fascinating.

61
A. Forestier, 1923
Illustrated London News, **10 February 1923**
Tourists at the excavation of King Tutankhamen's tomb, Valley of the Kings, Egypt

By the 1920s, classical archaeology had an enormous following in the Western world. Both drawings and photographic illustrations in the *Illustrated London News* (1923) of the opening of Tutankhamen's tomb captured **this public enthusiasm: "The incessant click of the ubiquitous Kodak, indeed, must be a sound as familiar there as the constant creaking of the crude waterwheels which abound in the locality."**

"Every person of culture and education lived through the drama of discovering Troy" in the 1870s, as daily newspapers increased their circulation by reporting Heinrich Schliemann's progress in excavating the seven-layered city (fig. 60) (White 1941:27). The reports "filtered into the consciousness of the age" (Deuel 1978:7–8). In 1847 Austen Henry Layard was advised by his close friend, Sir Charles Alison, to "write a whopper with lots of plates, fish up old legends and anecdotes, and if you can by any means humbug people into the belief that you have established any points in the Bible, you are a made man" (Waterfield 1963:171). Layard heeded his advice, and *Nineveh and its Remains* (1849) became the first archaeological bestseller in English. Although Layard never used photography, many others did: daguerreotypists were in the field within a year of Daguerre's invention, photographing the monuments of Egypt. In an age of robust imperial expansionism, new visual technologies were drawn on to both tap and feed the widespread excitement about earlier empires—Assyria, Egypt, Greece, Rome (fig. 61). Thousands would gladly pay to ponder their growth and decline, climb their monuments, and handle their treasures, even if only visually and vicariously.

By the 1880s the camera had become a tool of both public relations and professional service. There were notable failures as well as famous successes. For years Augustus and Alice Dixon Le Plongeon (Le Plongeon 1886) excavated in the jungles of Yucatán under trying conditions, scrupulously photographing their discoveries and publicizing their adventures through the museums, scientific institutions, and publishing houses of Europe and North America (fig. 62). They dreamed of fame and fortune through their archaeological research but died unacknowledged and in abject poverty. When W. M. Flinders Petrie, founder of the Egypt Exploration Fund in England, published his first archaeological handbook, *Methods and Aims of Archaeology* (1904), he allotted an entire chapter to excavation photography. In 1905, Harvard University and the Boston Museum of Fine Arts founded their own Egyptian Expedition under the direction of George A. Reisner, who also excavated in the Middle East for the Harvard Semitic Museum (fig. 63). For thirty years the Egyptian Expedition's periodic, detailed photographic reports of sites, excavations, and artifacts were the source of popular items in the journals and newspapers of the day.

62
Alice and Augustus Le Plongeon,
ca. 1873–1885
Albumen prints
Excerpts from photographic display boards

The Le Plongeons spent over twelve years in the jungles of Yucatán, single-mindedly devoting themselves to the discovery and photographic recording of Maya antiquities. Their "science" was on the fringe of the respectable archaeology of their day. Mystics and archaeological enthusiasts, the Le Plongeons sought to prove that the Maya civilization was the source of all metaphysical knowledge that later passed (via Atlantis) to the Egyptians and the Greeks. Born the Count de Coquerville, Le Plongeon spent his personal fortune on his research and produced an impressive photographic record. But he died destitute, his dream of establishing a school for students of American archaeology and esoteric wisdom unfulfilled.

FROM THE WILDS OF YUCATAN.

RUINS OF AKÉ.

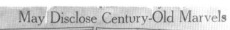

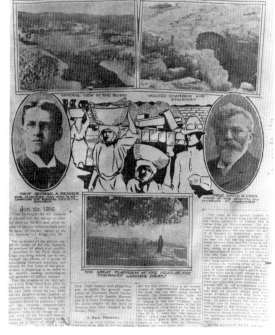

May Disclose Century-Old Marvels

63
The Boston Sunday *Post*, 30 January 1916

In the early years of the twentieth century, photography and drawing were still combined to illustrate popular accounts of archaeological exploits. The romance of Old World antiquities spawned and continued to support many major expeditions, like the Harvard Semitic Museum's excavations of the Biblical city of Samaria.

Digging the Ohio Mounds

Classical archaeology established a model for Americans, including the founders of the Peabody Museum. North American prehistory could hardly boast the impressive monuments of ancient Old World civilizations, although some patriotic Americans tried to equate the two. On 21 October 1868 Oliver Wendell Holmes wrote to Jeffries Wyman, first director of the Peabody Museum, that digs in the shell heaps of Maine and Florida "delight me . . . almost as it would to dredge the Tiber" (Wyman Papers). In fact, most archaelogy—whether on the shores of the Mediterranean or the Great Lakes—is not spectacular; it is hard work for mundane treasures. Frederic Ward Putnam, a later director of the museum, insisted that New World archaeology, unable to dazzle with aesthetic marvels, would be scientific or it would be nothing. In the early 1880s Putnam chose the Indian mounds of the Ohio River valley as the place to establish a scientific method for North American archaeology. "This will be the standard for all time to come," he wrote on 4 November 1882 to Charles Metz, his principal fieldworker in Ohio (Metz Papers). Espousing a cautious method of "trenching and slicing," he instructed his workers by mail and in person, urging careful photography at every stage of excavation (Metz Papers, 7 March 1884):

> *By the way I wish you would continue to keep a section of the big [Turner] mound perfect, so that I can photograph it when I get there in May. I wish you could let a mass stand that would give me a full view from top mound to the trench off the sector with the pits. Let a column stand where the trees are or just back of the old altar . . . So that the photo. would show all the layers. Can't this be done?*

Putnam took numerous glass-plate negatives of the Ohio mound work for several distinct purposes (fig. 64). They served as the source for line engravings for both professional and popular articles (fig. 65) and for lantern slides

64
Frederic Ward Putnam, 1887
Gelatin dry-plate negative
Excavation of Serpent Mound, Adams County, Ohio

Putnam and his collaborator Charles Metz photographically documented their excavations in southern Ohio in the 1880s. Putnam's successful campaign to save the Serpent Mound was aided by the publicity he generated with photographs and engravings made from them to illustrate popular articles. This glass-plate negative of a burial at Serpent Mound appeared as an engraving in *Century* (Putnam 1890) (fig. 65), a leading general-interest magazine of the day.

(fig. 66), with which he illustrated fund-raising lectures in the Boston area and in local Ohio communities. Putnam also used them for study, teaching, and exhibit in the museum. Recognizing the truth of the archaeological maxim that "to dig is to destroy," Putnam intended his photographs to serve as a means of visually preserving archaeological sites. Finally, the photographic record served as insurance against accusations of scientific fraud. For many years Putnam was embroiled in a nasty dispute over early man in North America (Meltzer 1983), an argument that hinged largely on the validity of field evidence and the integrity of fieldworkers. Under problematic professional conditions, on-site photography bolstered the credibility of untrained fieldworkers and protected Putnam and the Peabody Museum (Hinsley 1976).

*which we had carefully uncovered, and making
notes and drawing of the graves and their con-
tents, they believed in us, and with few exceptions
were ready to give their aid in various ways, and
offer us chances to dig on their lands."*

Frederic Ward Putnam to the Boston *Herald*
Peabody Museum Camp, Brown County, Ohio
20 September 1886

65
Century magazine, 1890
Line engraving from glass-plate negative
"Recent Indian grave, showing position of burial
over an ancient grave marked by the stones,"
Serpent Mound, Adams County, Ohio

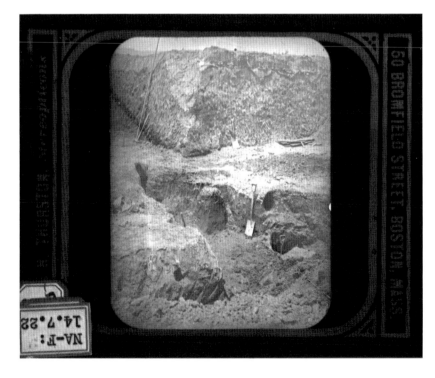

66
Frederic Ward Putnam(?), 1884
Lantern slide
Excavation of Turner Mound, Ohio

Putnam was the first
American archaeologist
to stress scrupulously
documented excava-
tion. Photographs of
his fieldwork attest to
both his scientific
methods and his con-
cern for visual records
of the work. He used
lantern slides, some-
times copied from
glass-plate negatives, to
illustrate professional,
popular, and classroom
lectures.

*"It has a curious attraction somehow. I have got
so that I am not content unless I am there. My
ambition is to get a mould and photograph every
piece in it before leaving it again."*

**George Byron Gordon to Charles P. Bowditch
Copán, Honduras, 20 May 1895**

Seeing Copán: Visual Records and Reconstruction

In 1891 the Peabody Museum took the archaeological camera to Copán, Honduras. Operating
under a ten-year concession from the Honduran
government, John G. Owens and Marshall
Saville arrived in December and began to excavate and photograph the impressive monuments
of the Classic Maya site. On 23 January 1893,
three weeks before his sudden death in the
field, Owens wrote to Charles P. Bowditch,
trustee of the Peabody Museum, "My work on
Mound #26 is revealing what must have been a
most magnificent sculptured stairway on the
western slope of the mound" (Bowditch Papers).
George Byron Gordon continued Owens's work
on the crumbled stairway (fig. 67), carefully
digging away at the hillside. "It has a curious
attraction somehow," he ruminated in a letter to
Bowditch dated 20 May 1895. "I have got so
that I am not content unless I am there. My

ambition now is to get a mould and photograph
every piece in it before leaving it again"
(Bowditch Papers).

Gordon documented the stages of his work with
dozens of photographs, as he lifted the stones
with a hoist (fig. 68), moved them by oxcart,
and laid them out in the courtyard (fig. 69). His
goal was to record them so that they could "be
reproduced in the Museum at Cambridge for
further investigation and study" (Gordon
1896:8). So little was known about Maya hieroglyphic writing at the time that there was no
way to reconstruct the original sequence of the
stairway with any certainty, and numerous
pieces were left stacked about the courtyard.
When Sylvanus G. Morley visited the site for
the Carnegie Institution of Washington, D.C.,
more than two decades later, he reported that
the "wreckage of America's greatest aboriginal
effort in the science of writing" still lay in

67
Photographer unknown, 1893
Gelatin dry-plate negative
**Mound 26 in the early stages of clearing for
excavation of the Hieroglyphic Stairway, Peabody
Museum Second Honduras Expedition, Copán**

In 1893 the Peabody
Museum's Second Hon-
duras Expedition at
Copán discovered and
began excavating a
magnificent stairway of
2,500 sculptured hiero-
glyphic blocks.
Gordon took over ex-
cavation of the stairway
after John G. Owens's
untimely death in the
field and devised a

hoist-and-pully
method for extracting
and lowering the heavy
blocks. The loose
stones were laid out on
the plaza in front of the
mound. Gordon's ex-
tensive visual record
was at least in part a
product of Putnam's
influence and Charles
P. Bowditch's generous
funding.

"inextricable confusion" in the plaza (Morley 1920:241). "Indeed," Morley wrote (ibid.:vi),

> no exhaustive study of the Copán inscriptions could have been completed without recourse to the rich collections in the Peabody Museum, not only of original sculptures and casts, but also of hundreds of early unpublished photographs.

As Morley intimated, the Copán expedition's visual record has proved to be exceedingly valuable. Because of the destruction and erosion suffered by the excavated stones, the original pictures are our only means of seeing the glyphs as they first emerged. They serve also as valuable corroborative evidence for the field notes of the early investigators (Gordon Willey 1985: personal communication). In the late 1930s, when the Carnegie Institution decided to sort out and rebuild the 2,500-glyph-block stairway, its archaeologists acknowledged that the undertaking could not have been carried out without the original Peabody expedition notes and photographs (Carnegie Institution 1937:4). Knowledge of the hieroglyphs was still so partial that some stones were cemented together in the wrong order, but the reconstructed stairway nonetheless gave a fair sense of the majesty of the original (fig. 70).

The Copán photographs also reached the public at an opportune time. In its first two field seasons the Peabody expedition produced approximately five hundred photographs of the operations and site. Of these, 162 were displayed—along with Central American photographs by Alfred P. Maudslay and molds of stelae and other monuments from Yucatán, Copán, and Quiriguá—at the World's Columbian Exposition in Chicago in 1893. This striking exhibit, the first major display of Maya architecture in the United States, convinced millions of fairgoers that New World archaeology could be a source of pride, worthy of attention and perhaps investment.

68
Photographer unknown, 1895
Gelatin dry-plate negative
Removing fallen sculptured blocks from the Hieroglyphic Stairway, Peabody Museum Fourth Honduras Expedition, Copán

69
Photographer unknown, 1893–1895
Gelatin dry-plate negative
Loose steps from the Hieroglyphic Stairway laid out in plaza in front of mound, Peabody Museum Fourth Honduras Expedition, Copán

70
Photographer unknown, ca. 1940
Gelatin silver print
Hieroglyphic Stairway after restoration by
Carnegie Institution of Washington, D.C.

When the Carnegie In-
stitution decided to re-
build the stairway, the
Peabody Museum's
photographic archive
provided an invaluable
resource. The restora-
tion was undertaken
between 1937 and

1940 under the direc-
tion of Sylvanus G.
Morley. Archaeologists
still turn to these early
photographs for infor-
mation about Copán
and the first systematic
excavations at the site.

A Bird's-Eye View of Prehistory:
Aerial Photography

Until the early twentieth century, archaeological
discovery was largely a result of field survey,
excavation, and luck. The airplane made broad
reconnaissance feasible for the first time, and
aerial photography made possible techniques of
observation that could bring to the surface previously obscured features. Military interests always played a central role: the first aerial
photographs of an archaeological site were
taken in 1906 from a military balloon over
Stonehenge by Lieutenant P. H. Sharpe (Capper
1907). The First World War gave impetus to
aerial photography for both military and non-
military purposes and led to experimentation
and rapid development in the principles of aerial archaeology during the 1920s and 1930s.
Most of this pioneering activity took place in
England and France. O. G. S. Crawford and
Alexander Keiller's *Wessex from the Air* (1928)
and Antoine Poidebard's *La trace de Rome dans
le désert de Syrie* (1934), among many other
works of the period, brilliantly demonstrated the
versatility of the aerial camera in locating and
elucidating man-made structures.

In 1921 the Indian mounds of Cahokia, Illinois,
became the first North American archaeological
sites to be photographed from the air. In general, American archaeologists remained unim-
pressed by the new technique until 1929, when
Charles and Anne Morrow Lindbergh undertook
two highly publicized reconnaissance flights
(fig. 71) (Carnegie Institution 1929; Kidder
1929): in August over the Pueblo region of the
southwestern United States and in October
over parts of British Honduras (now Belize),
Guatemala, and the Yucatán peninsula. The
Lindberghs demonstrated that topographical and
ecological features relevant to the prehistory of
the region could be detected from the air in
terrain that permits easy visibility of ruins
(Carnegie Institution 1929:113).

Sponsored by Pan American Airways and the
Carnegie Institution of Washington, D.C., the
second Lindbergh effort aimed at both a comprehensive regional view and discovery of individual sites. Alfred V. Kidder, director of

archaeology for the Carnegie Institution and later curator of North American archaeology and ethnology at the Peabody Museum, accompanied the Lindberghs "to test the aeroplane as an agency for archaeological exploration in tropical countries . . . [and] to gain a comprehensive understanding of the real nature of this territory" (Kidder 1930:194–195).

The Lindberghs' excursion in Central America was characteristically bold and flashy, but it bore meager results. The team used the camera only as an adjunct to eye observation (fig. 72), without employing any of the detective capabilities or diagnostic principles of aerial photography, such as direction and intensity of light, shadow length, and angle of viewing. Despite its scientific barrenness, the Middle American reconnaissance of Kidder and the Lindberghs publicized aerial archaeology in the New World as never before (fig. 73).

Kidder's yearning for a "comprehensive understanding" of Maya country expressed a new consensus among American archaeologists on the need for regional syntheses. The Lower Mississippi Survey (LMS), headquartered at the Peabody Museum, has embodied the regional survey tradition of the past half century, and aerial photography has been one of its central techniques. The LMS was founded in 1939 by Philip Phillips, curator of southeastern American archaeology in the Peabody Museum, James A. Ford of Louisiana State University, and James B. Griffin of the University of Michigan. It employs various kinds of aerial photography to record archaeological site patterning in those areas of the Mississippi flood plain where the meandering river has brought about large-scale site destruction. Seminal research during the Second World War by Louisiana geologist Harold N. Fisk, who traced the changing channels of the Mississippi through analysis of aerial photographs (Fisk 1944), led to correlations between prehistoric sites and earlier river patterns (Phillips, Ford, and Griffin 1951:295). Currently under the direction of archaeologist Stephen Williams, the LMS is now working with more than fifty years of aerial photographs and maps that go back as far as the seventeenth century.

71
Oliver G. Ricketson, Jr., 1929
Black-and-white negative
Charles and Anne Morrow Lindbergh in the cockpit of their airplane during the Carnegie Institution's survey of the Maya regions

The Lindberghs took to the air in this twin-engine Sikorsky amphibion, donated by Pan American Airways, during the first aerial survey of the Maya regions of Central America. They were accompanied by anthropologists Alfred V. Kidder and Oliver G. Ricketson, Jr.

72
Anne Morrow Lindbergh, 1929
Black-and-white negative
Aerial view of Chichén Itzá, Mexico

The Lindberghs' survey relied on the naked eye and the work of amateur photographers: the camera was used only to confirm and record what the aviators could see. The well-known site of Chichén Itzá in northern Yucatán was already cleared and excavated and, hence, visible from the air when the Lindberghs flew over. Previously unknown sites are usually so obscured by dense jungle that aerial detection requires the sophisticated survey technologies devised during the twenties and thirties by military pilots and engineers in England and France.

73
Saturday Evening Post, 11 January 1930

The Lindberghs were more successful in promoting the use of aerial photography in archaeology than in producing scientific results for the Carnegie Institution of Washington, D.C., which, along with Pan American Airways, sponsored their survey of the Maya region.

EXPLORING THE MAYA WITH LINDBERGH—By William I. Van Dusen

BLAZING an aerial highway northward since the first air mail from Panama to the United States, Col. Charles A. Lindbergh came upon one of the mystic, jungle-covered cities of the Mayas. Buried deep in the virgin bush of Eastern Yucatan, the unnatural-shaped mounds were first sighted by the flyer's companion, Col. John A. Hambleton, while scouting far off their original course to chart possible auxiliary landing fields.

The sight of that forgotten city, deserted since the time of the people who built it, stimulated Colonel Lindbergh's interest in the possibility of aerial surveys to assist scientists in their study of the Maya land, so difficult to penetrate from the ground. Out of that incident came the first aerial exploration into the

our various trips to Belize, and then Lindbergh and the scientists immediately set to work on the final projection of the flights. Tracing the outlines on the maps, Kidder and Ricketson summarized the territory to be covered.

From the Gulf of Mexico southward to the volcanic peaks of Nicaragua, the savage tropic jungle, unstayed by the hand of man, has swallowed up all but a few blurred pages in the history of a once mighty race. Following the meager, hazardous trails of the *chicleros*, who cut their way through the jungle with machetes in search of the valuable chicle, scientists have located several of the great Mayan capitals. From them has been pieced together the little we know of that marvelous civilization which flourished in Ame-

Cozumel, One of Aviation's Outposts. On This Island Airport Builders Uncovered Part of a Maya City

"As its methods and techniques are improved, aerial photography will increase in scientific value. In the not distant future, it will become an indispensable adjunct to field work."

Dache M. Reeves, 1936
"Aerial Photography and Archaeology"

74
United States Department of the Interior, 1949
Black-and-white aerial photograph
Lake George site, Yazoo County, Mississippi

At Lake George in the Yazoo Basin of the lower Mississippi River, the LMS for many years has been reconstructing the pattern of past settlements (Phillips 1970; Williams and Brain 1983). An aerial view of the Lake George site (fig. 74) was the source of the 1949 topographic map in figure 75. Aerial photography of the Mississippi River valley (fig. 76) reveals topographical striations that indicate past currents of movement in the meander belt of the river. Physiographic reconstruction of the basin shows the current and past positions of the river, with the historic sites of the time marked along its course (fig. 77). LMS archaeologists have also used infrared aerial views to detect areas of past human habitation along the river (fig. 78).

The result of the Lower Mississippi Survey work is a reconstruction of past geological and cultural landscapes. It also stands as a reminder that the pressures of industrial and demographic change, along with the whims of nature, threaten to obliterate not only the ancient past but recent history as well. The broad perspective afforded by aerial photography enables us to assess changing conditions so that we may apply the limited resources of archaeology most efficiently to the endangered remains of human cultures all around us (Deuel 1969:295–298).

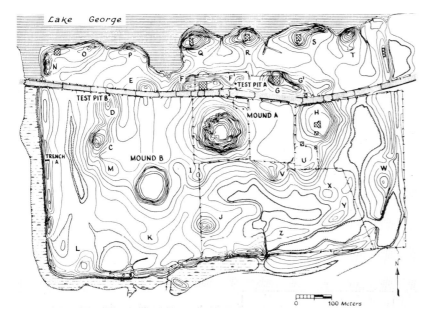

75
A. C. Spaulding, 1949
Topographic map based on aerial photograph
Lake George site, Yazoo County, Mississippi

Aerial and ground surveys are complementary. Features detected from the air require ground survey for confirmation, and vice versa.

76
United States Department of the Interior, 1960
Black-and-white aerial photographs
Lake St. Joseph, Tensas Parish, Louisiana

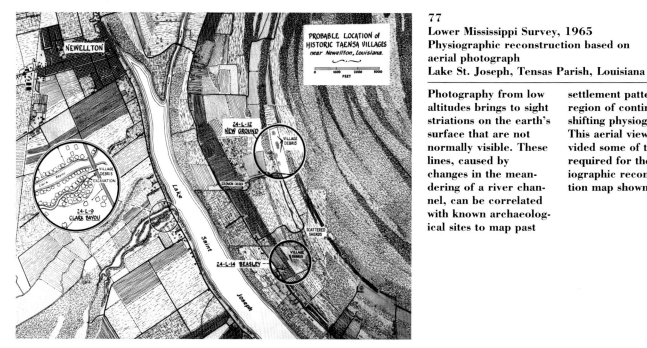

77
Lower Mississippi Survey, 1965
Physiographic reconstruction based on
aerial photograph
Lake St. Joseph, Tensas Parish, Louisiana

Photography from low altitudes brings to sight striations on the earth's surface that are not normally visible. These lines, caused by changes in the meandering of a river channel, can be correlated with known archaeological sites to map past settlement patterns in a region of continually shifting physiography. This aerial view provided some of the data required for the physiographic reconstruction map shown here.

78
Louisiana Office of State Parks, 1980
Color infrared aerial photograph
Mississippi River valley, West Feliciana Parish,
Louisiana

Infrared radiation has longer wavelengths than those at the red end of the visible light spectrum. For archaeologists, infrared photography is particularly useful for recording sites of past human occupation not ordinarily visible. The intensity of the red tones in the cleared field discloses a higher organic content than that of the surrounding soil, indicating (in this instance) the location of a former human habitation.

The View from Within: Microphotography and Archaeology

For political and technological reasons, archaeologists are turning renewed attention to existing museum collections. "Indeed," predicts one writer on archaeological ethics, "the day may come when most of the data are in museums rather than in the ground" (Green 1984:133). Techniques of microanalysis provide abundant data on recent discoveries and let us view older museum collections with fresh eyes.

The Mecklenburg Collection at the Peabody Museum comes from four Early Iron Age grave groups in Hallstatt, Austria, and what is now the Yugoslav Republic of Slovenia. It represents one of the earliest ironworking cultures outside of the classical world. Between 1905 and 1914, the Duchess of Mecklenburg (born Princess Maria von Windischgrätz of Austria) excavated about a thousand graves in the cemeteries of Hallstatt, Stična, Magdalenska gora,

and Vinica. While her records, including photographs of the excavation (fig. 79), were relatively complete for the time, the Duchess never undertook a systematic study of the grave goods. When the entire collection came up for sale in New York in 1934, Hugh Hencken, curator of European archaeology at the Peabody Museum and director of prehistoric studies in the American School of Prehistoric Research, arranged for the museum to acquire the materials. He published two bulletins on his research of the collection (1968, 1978), and his student Peter Wells followed up with further studies (Wells 1981). Thus, by the time of the first comprehensive study of the Mecklenburg materials, they had been out of the ground for over fifty years.

In that half century the theoretical and methodological contours of European prehistory had altered dramatically. In the Duchess's time, the accepted technological divisions of European prehistoric archaeology—Stone, Bronze, and

79
Photographer unknown, 1907
Black-and-white negative
Duchess of Mecklenburg supervising excavations
Hallstatt, Austria

The Duchess of Mecklenburg directly supervised excavations in Iron Age cemeteries in Austria and Slovenia in the decade before the First World War, on occasion even wielding a pick. The photographs of the excavation, rare in European archaeology of the time, hold vital information about the process of discovery and the sites themselves: local topography, working conditions at the site, *in situ* aspects of the grave goods, and locations of the graves in relation to each other. The artifact collections are now being studied by advanced photoanalytic methods. The power of this technical analysis must be complemented by every effort to place the artifacts in their original context, especially where sites have drastically changed over time or disappeared altogether.

Iron ages—were only general categories. By 1960, the influence of social and cultural anthropology had begun to be felt strongly in archaeology, as witnessed by new interest in social organization, community size, economic classes, and the relationship between natural resources and technological innovation. In response to these new concerns, archaeologists recently have borrowed techniques from the natural and physical sciences, including some involving photography. In 1980 the Peabody Museum opened the Center for Archaeological Research and Development (CARD), which integrates a number of laboratories capable of analyzing the complete range of archaeological materials. Photography is a key element of CARD's metallographic laboratory.

The complex structure of an artifact is a record of its past. By careful scrutiny, archaeometallurgists can derive information about the point of origin of raw materials and how they were obtained and traded. The ways in which materials were processed, combined, and finished indicate the degree of technical expertise required to produce the artifact, allowing the archaeometallurgist to deduce specialization of production and levels of social complexity.

The Mecklenburg collection is currently being reanalyzed in the CARD laboratory by students and faculty. The photoanalysis of a more than two-thousand-year-old iron knife by graduate student Michael Geselowitz demonstrates the wealth of information obtainable from a single object (fig. 80). A section cut from the edge of the corroded knife blade reveals any surviving metal inside (fig. 81). Under an optical microscope, even at a relatively low power of magnification, two distinctly different zones in the knife can be seen and recorded for further analysis in a photomicrograph (fig. 82). Under greater magnification, it becomes clear that two different pieces of metal were forged together to make this small tool (fig. 83).

80
Hillel Burger, 1985
Black-and-white negative
Iron knife from the Mecklenburg collection
with sample cross section removed

Materials in the Mecklenburg collection come from one of the earliest known ironworking cultures outside of the classical	**world. Archaeologists estimate this iron knife to be approximately 2,000 years old.**

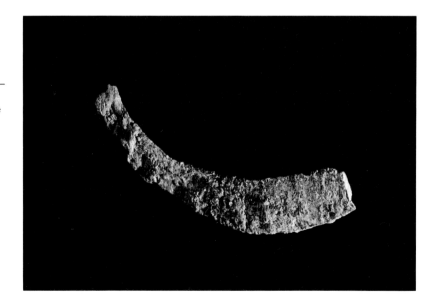

*"Indeed the day may come when most of the data
are in museums rather than in the ground."*

Ernestene L. Green, 1984
Ethics and Values in Archaeology

Because of the characteristic wavelength of
light, there are limits to the resolution of optical
microscopy. Therefore another photomicro-
graphic technique, scanning electron microscopy (SEM), which "illuminates" the specimen
with electrons rather than visible light, is used
(fig. 84). SEM reveals a microscopic structure,
pearlite, which indicates that the edge of the
knife was turned into steel through the introduction of carbon. The Iron Age smith had apparently learned to produce a harder, more
brittle edge by holding iron for some time in a
charcoal fire. The combination is ideal: the
steel provides a fine cutting edge, and the softer
iron back, which can bear a high degree of
strain, makes it less likely to snap. The quality
of production of this tool confirms recent research demonstrating the highly developed art
of the late-prehistoric European smith.

CARD's metallographic laboratory is able to retrieve from artifacts a previously unimagined
amount of data with far-reaching interpretive
possibilities. This power of analysis demands
that every effort be made to place the artifact in
its original setting, and the Duchess's photographs provide this contextual information. In
short, rather than supplanting conventional photographic methods, sophisticated photoanalysis
makes them all the more critical.

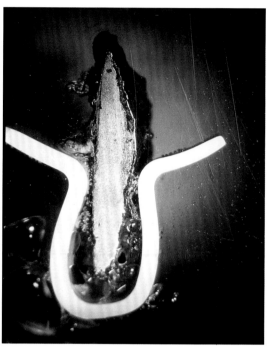

81
Michael Geselowitz, 1985
Color transparency
Cross section of tip of iron knife

Although the knife is
highly corroded on the
outside, a cross section
reveals the surviving
metal inside.

82
Michael Geselowitz, 1985
Color photomicrograph
Iron knife photographed at 12.5 times
magnification

Once the knife is
properly prepared, the
researcher examines it
with an optical micro-
scope. With the aid of
a reflecting mirror, a
camera records the
magnified image for
further study. Even at
this relatively low
power of magnification,
two distinct zones in
the knife come into
view. On the left, the
metal contains many
small, nonmetallic "in-
clusions" and has large
light-colored grains.
Fewer nonmetallic in-
clusions appear on the
right, where smaller
light-colored grains are
interspersed with
darker grains that are
more numerous at the
edge and tip of the
blade. Higher magnifi-
cation is needed to ex-
amine the difference
between these two
zones.

83
Michael Geselowitz, 1985
Color photomicrograph
Iron knife photographed at 40 times magnification

The craftsmanship of this tool is very fine, but this degree of magnification reveals a line where two pieces of metal were imperfectly joined. In addition to providing a record of analysis, the photomicrograph enables the researcher to measure such things as the percentage of nonmetallic inclusions, which gives some idea of the metal's quality. Fewer inclusions on the right represent a more refined iron composition, indicating that this section was carefully worked to remove nonmetallic particles. The left zone, which is less worked and refined, has elongated inclusions.

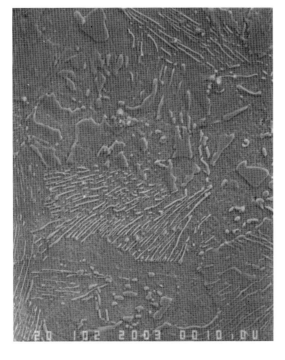

84
Michael Geselowitz, 1985
Scanning electron micrograph (SEM)
Instant black-and-white print of iron knife at 1,000 times magnification

SEM "illuminates" the specimen with electrons that have shorter wavelengths than visible light and can "see" even smaller detail than the optical microscope. Projected onto a cathode ray tube (TV screen), the resultant image is copied by means of an instant print. The fine bands visible here represent the microscopic structure of pearlite, indicating that carbon was introduced into the iron on the edge of the knife to produce the harder compound, steel.

"To Copy the Millions of Hieroglyphics": Photography and Epigraphy

While photographic microanalysis of artifacts goes forward in museum laboratories, improved photographic techniques also contribute to epigraphy, the recording and interpretation of inscriptions. The idea of applying photography to epigraphy is as old as photography itself, for hand-copying inscriptions from rock faces, large and detailed sculptures, or high monuments was indeed laborious. During the 1840s Austen Henry Layard worked eighteen-hour days drawing and copying. "You have no idea of the extreme tediousness of copying them . . . the patience of the most exemplary of the Patriarchs would be exhausted," he wrote (Waterfield 1963:124). From the deserts of the Middle East to the Yucatán jungles, epigraphists had two things in common: determination and discomfort. Henry C. Rawlinson, a pioneer in cuneiform translation, and other archaeologists spent hours in uncomfortable positions, hanging by ropes or perched on precarious scaffolding, to copy otherwise inaccessible writing. It is hardly surprising that in 1839 François Arago, secretary of the French Academy of Sciences and the most influential French scientist of his day, had the prescience to write of the virtues of the new art of photography as a time- and labor-saving invention for science (Taft 1938:5–6; Vaczek and Buckland 1981:34).

Maya epigraphy has had a remarkably continuous tradition over the past hundred fifty years. On his first Central American trip with explorer and author John Lloyd Stephens in 1839, illustrator Frederick Catherwood took along a *camera lucida* for tracing images (fig. 85). Developed in 1807, the camera lucida reflected an image of an object or scene onto a drawing surface from which the operator, looking through the glass prism of the device, could trace it. For his second excursion, in 1841 to Yucatán, Catherwood purchased a daguerreotype outfit with which, in spite of numerous failures, he created some images that were reproduced as engravings. The illustrations in both sets of *Incidents of Travel* (Stephens 1841, 1843) helped create their enormous popularity. In ensuing years growing public and scientific interest in Maya culture produced ever more insistent demands for accuracy in illustration, and this could be satisfied best through photography.

Political unrest in the region may explain the absence over the next twenty years of serious effort to gather additional data about the ruins. Then in 1857 the French government sent a young traveller named Désiré Charnay, who was also a highly skilled photographer, to photograph ruins in Mexico (fig. 86). He came with a huge camera and a supply of glass plates, the safety of which was a constant source of preoccupation as the pack-mule carrying them lurched through rough country. Despite these difficulties and the continued political turmoil of the area, Charnay produced magnificent images.

Alfred Maudslay, the English archaeologist, mapped and photographed Copán, Quiriguá, Tikal, Yaxchilán, Chichén Itzá, and Palenque (fig. 87). He was the first archaeologist to study Yaxchilán, on the Usumacinta River, arriving there in 1882 only a few days before Charnay. Maudslay was also the first to realize that however exquisite and accurate they might be, "photographs of elaborate sculpture and hieroglyphic inscriptions are not by themselves adequate for scholarly purposes, but need to be supplemented by drawings" (Graham n.d.:8). His archaeological photography and an accompanying text were published in large format as five volumes of the series *Biologia centraliamericana* (Maudslay 1899–1902), with drawings made from plaster casts printed beside the photographs. As Maudslay understood, some details can be seen more clearly with the naked eye. Others, of barely perceptible relief, can be brought out and (today) photographed with controlled illumination. A century ago, this was not feasible. Maudslay's solution was to take molds of sculpture, have plaster casts made from them in England, and employ trained artists to make line drawings under conditions that permitted some control of lighting. The drawings of each monument would then be published alongside the photographs of it.

"He was standing with his feet in the mud, and was drawing with his gloves on to protect his hands from the moschetoes. As we feared, the designs [on the monuments of Copán] were so intricate and complicated, the subjects so entirely new and unintelligible, that he had great difficulty in drawing. He had made several attempts, both with the camera lucida and without, but failed to satisfy himself or even me, who was less severe in criticism. The 'idol' seemed to defy his art; two monkeys on a tree on one side appeared to be laughing at him, and I felt discouraged and despondent. In fact, I made up my mind, with a pang of regret, that we must abandon the idea of carrying away any materials for antiquarian speculation, and must be content with having seen them ourselves. Of that satisfaction nothing could deprive us."

John Lloyd Stephens, 1841
Incidents of Travel in Central America, Chiapas and Yucatan

85
Frederick Catherwood, 1839–1840 (published 1844)
Lithograph from original sepia drawing
Idol and altar, Copán, Honduras

Despite the availability of photographic technology on Catherwood and John Lloyd Stephens's second expedition to Central America in 1841–1842, Stephens noted that Catherwood continued, as on their first expedition, to make "all his drawings with the camera lucida, for the purpose of obtaining the utmost accuracy of proportion and detail. Besides which, we had with us a Daguerreotype apparatus... with which, immediately on our arrival at Uxmal, Mr. Catherwood began taking views; but the results were not sufficiently perfect to suit his ideas. At times the projecting cornices and ornaments threw parts of the subject in shade, while others were in broad sunshine; so that, while parts were brought out well, other parts required pencil drawings to supply their defects. . . . He therefore completed everything with his pencil and camera lucida while Doctor Cabot and myself took up the Daguerreotype; and, in order to ensure the utmost accuracy, the Daguerreotype views were placed with the drawings in the hands of the engravers for their guidance" (Stephens 1843[I]:99–100).

86
Désiré Charnay, 1860
Albumen print
The prison, Chichén Itzá, Mexico

After Charnay success-
fully turned his camera
on the ruins of Yucatán
in 1857, the value of
photographic documen-
tation of the monu-
ments of ancient
America was estab-
lished. Not a man of
scholarly temperament,
Charnay is more aptly
described as a popular-
izer, lively travel
writer, and superb pho-
tographer with a strong
interest in antiquities.
Folio-size prints of his
negatives were pub-
lished in his *Cités et
ruines américanes:
Mitla, Palenqué, Iza-
mal, Chichen-Itza,
Uxmal* (1862–1863),
accompanied by a
smaller volume of text.

87
Alfred P. Maudslay, 1891
Albumen print
North face of the tower in the palacio before
excavation, Palenque, Mexico

Maudslay, a man of
great practical ability
as a photographer and
surveyor, showed sound
judgment in his general
approach to the prob-
lems of a developing
discipline. He made
seven expeditions to
Central America be-
tween 1881 and 1894,
in the course of which
he mapped, photo-
graphed, made plaster
casts, and sometimes
excavated at numerous
ruins.

Another early photographer of Maya sites was Teobert Maler. Son of a German military officer, Maler joined the Austrian Pioneer Company for service in Mexico under Emperor Maximilian. He returned to Mexico in 1884 and during his time there worked along the Usumacinta River and in Petén, Guatemala. Maler, who had some training in architecture, was a superb photographer and darkroom technician who for many years travelled through Central America in search of ruins to photograph, measure, and describe. At one point he planned to produce a great illustrated atlas of Central American antiquities, which he hoped to sell by subscription at great profit. This scheme fell through, and in 1897 Maler began a ten-year collaboration with the Peabody Museum that yielded valuable volumes in its Memoirs series (1901–1903, 1908, 1910, 1911). Among them were the first reports on such sites as Piedras Negras, Seibal, and Naranjo as well as studies of Tikal and Yaxchilán.

Maler first visited Yaxchilán in 1895. He returned for several months in 1897 and completed his work there for the museum in early 1900, making paper molds and photographing extensively on this last visit (fig. 88). Maler's photographs are dazzling accomplishments. He used flexible film for the Peabody assignment, which enabled him to photograph relief sculptures in several pieces and assemble photomosaics of them. All his negatives were developed on site, and subsequent printing was done at his home in Yucatán. "The results he obtained

88
Teobert Maler, ca. 1897
Black-and-white negative
Lintel 26, Yaxchilán, Mexico

For his fieldwork in the tropical forest, Maler used flexible negatives instead of glass plates. The danger of breakage thus was eliminated, and he was able to compose photomosaics of monuments found in several pieces, like Lintel 26 at the Maya site of Yaxchilán.

By photographing each fragment at the same distance, thus at the same scale, he could simply cut the image area from each negative and assemble the pieces on a transparent sheet in their correct relative positions, ready for reproduction.

89
Sylvanus G. Morley, 1931
Black-and-white negative
Lintel 26, Yaxchilán, Mexico

In some instances, one photographer's work may not provide all the visual documentation needed for complete examination of a piece of sculpture. Morley, who had great appreciation of the value of the photographic record, made his own images of Lintel 26 many years after Maler. Photographic documentation of the same subject at different points in time enriches our understanding of archaeological and historic sites and monuments.

90
Ian Graham, 1977
Line drawings
Lintel 26, Yaxchilán, Mexico

Parts of Lintel 26 have eroded badly since Maler's day, and Graham's recent drawings of the stone inscription are based in part on Mal-	**er's and Morley's photographs. Their images serve as primary sources of information for Maya epigraphists.**

in such a hot climate and in a primitive darkroom do him the greatest credit" (Graham n.d.:10).

The work of Sylvanus Morley represents another period of photographic research in Central America (fig. 89). Having interested the Carnegie Institution in Maya archaeology, Morley spent over twenty years in Central America under its auspices, publishing *The Inscriptions at Copan* in 1920 and *The Inscriptions of Peten* in 1937–1938. Although not as brilliant as the work of his predecessors, Morley's photographic record remains valuable for the research of epigraphers today.

The search for greater fidelity in recording Maya writing is carried on by Ian Graham of the Peabody Museum. Relying on his own drawings and on-site photographs and the photographic corpus of his predecessors, Graham, in collaboration with Eric von Euw and Peter Mathews, over the last decade has published eleven parts of a projected fifty in the authoritative *Corpus of Maya Hieroglyphic Inscriptions* (1975–   ). Graham notes that the advantage of drawing is that "details visible in several different photographs, none of which by itself shows all of them, can be combined into one rendering" (1985: personal communication). Graham's drawings of Lintel 26 at Yaxchilán (fig. 90) are based partly on photographs taken by Maler in 1900 (see fig. 88) and Morley in 1931 (see fig. 89). In the spirit of Maudslay, Graham combines the artistry of Catherwood with the precision of Maler for unprecedented detail in his epigraphic studies (fig. 91).

91
Otis Imboden, 1975
Color transparency
Ian Graham inspecting stela, Yaxchilán, Mexico

From the days of Catherwood, the dark forest canopy of Central America has posed serious problems of lighting for drawing or photographing Maya monuments. Graham inspects the relief on a stone sculpture at Yaxchilán preparatory to photographing it under strong artificial light.

Applying Photogrammetry to Epigraphy

As the Yaxchilán photo-drawings illustrate, it is critical in epigraphy to capture depth in order to bring out relief without distortion. Stereophotography is commonly employed for this purpose, and today the technique is being enhanced by the application of photogrammetry. The linking of photography with the study of epigraphy is not new: pictures of Egyptian hieroglyphs were taken as early as the 1840s, and *The Talbotype Applied to Hieroglyphics* was published in 1846. The potential of photogrammetry was also grasped virtually at the birth of photography. On the day that he announced Daguerre's invention to the world, Arago also predicted that photographic images, "abiding by the rules of geometry, will allow us, with the help of a small number of given facts, to reveal the exact dimensions of the highest, most inaccessible parts" of the great monuments of the classical world (Vaczek and Buckland 1981:34).

As applied to archaeology today, photogrammetry works on the principles of optics and geometry, using stereo pairs of two-dimensional photographs to record the true measures and forms of three-dimensional physical data. These stereophotographs are taken under carefully controlled conditions. When viewed side by side using a special optical device (a stereoscope), a three-dimensional image springs into view. Measurements can then be made of any features and processed to give the actual dimensions of the objects portrayed. In effect, stereophotographs add the depth dimension that is absent in ordinary two-dimensional photographs.

The technique came into wide use in archaeology only in the 1960s, when archaeologists began to have access to stereophotogrammetric equipment for accurate plotting of maps. Most of these systems were very expensive (Saley and Beale 1985:4), although it is possible to improvise relatively inexpensive photogrammetric setups in the field (Whittlesey 1975). In recent years archaeologists have used the method to survey and map large areas, single sites, and individual layers of an excavation; it is especially valuable in underwater archaeology (Rosencrantz 1975). In an innovative study, Margaret Blackman (1981) has supplemented archaeological data with photogrammetric analysis of historic photographs to reconstruct the architecture and interior features of a Haida house. In all its anthropological applications, photogrammetry is a valuable time- and labor-saving technique.

Photogrammetry is currently being used to study inscriptions on ancient tablets. In 1983 the American Schools of Oriental Research, a consortium of institutions, began to design a pioneering computerized photogrammetric system for archaeologists and epigraphists. Thomas Wight Beale, a research associate at the Peabody Museum, has been closely involved with the project. Beale, who worked on excavations at Tepe Yahya in southeastern Iran with C. C. Lamberg-Karlovsky, professor of anthropology at Harvard, is using computer-photogrammetry to study inscriptions on Proto-Elamite tablets from the site of Susa, Iran.

The oblong tablets of unbaked brown clay, dating to about 3,000 B.C., are inscribed from right to left, beginning at the top (fig. 92). Thought to be accounts of taxation or redistribution of goods among kinship groups, they could provide clues to units of economic production, local kinship networks, and the administrative apparatus of the Proto-Elamites. Instead of painstakingly transcribing the inscriptions by hand like a traditional epigraphist (Scheil 1923: tablet 97) (fig. 93), Beale scans the tablets much as one would map terrain from the air, using photogrammetry on a microscale. The data are taken along three coordinates (horizontal, vertical, and depth) and then digitized to produce computer graphics.

The picture that is presented on the computer screen differs from conventional epigraphy in both purposes and results (fig. 94). Traditional epigraphists sought to establish a standard language from the glyphs and tended to produce an idealized version of what they saw, possibly losing in variety what was gained in system. Microscale photogrammetry reveals not only the surface outlines of glyphs but also the depth of incisions into the clay and sequence of strokes, yielding information about the type of writing implements used and variations in style. With this data it may be possible to identify the hand of individual scribes, almost as one would analyze handwriting today. In short, the new method focuses attention on historically specific elements, the subtle variations in technique and style that escape the human eye but not the eye of the stereocamera and the digital computer.

"Only to a limited degree can you make distinctions of detail from traditional drawings. My idea first was to take good photographs and second to find a technology where I could use photography to redraw these tablets."

Thomas Wight Beale, 1985

92
Thomas Wight Beale, 1985
Black-and-white negative, one of a pair of stereophotographs
Proto-Elamite tablet from Susa, Iran

This oblong tablet of unbaked brown clay dates to about 3,000 B.C. and is thought to be an accounting ledger.

93
Textes de comptabilité proto-Élamites, 1923
Line drawing
Proto-Elamite tablet

The inscriptions on cuneiform tablets were studied first by means of traditional line drawings such as this one (Scheil 1923: tablet 97), which generally presented idealized versions of the glyphs, diminishing inconsistencies and variation in quest of a consistent language and orthography.

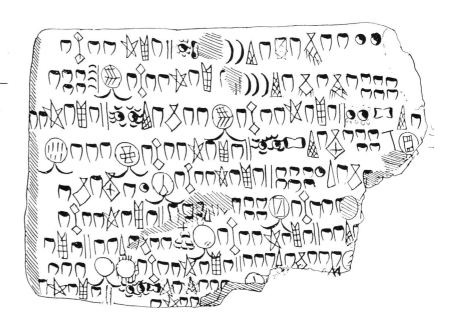

Archaeologists do not carry precisely the same ethical burdens as anthropologists who photograph living peoples. Yet they must consider equally problematic issues when digging up the human remains and artifacts of past cultures, issues that in a postcolonial world have been raised more frequently. Archaeologists cannot excavate certain Native American graves without tribal permission and observation or remove skeletons and grave goods without proper tribal ceremony and disposition (Green 1984). It has become more difficult to remove artifacts from their country of origin, and many museums are now addressing the question of repatriation of collections. These circumstances enhance the value of the photograph, which may constitute the only visual evidence brought back from the field.

Jacques Ellul, the French philosopher and social critic, some years ago warned Western societies against devolving into a mass culture of mere technique, in which feasibility studies and technical prowess decide not merely sociopolitical issues but moral judgments as well (Ellul 1964). The deep-rooted humanistic goals of archaeology are its most treasured tradition. The power of photography has enabled archaeologists to explore and even celebrate the commonality of humanity. Laboratory analysis of the artistry of an Iron Age smith, aerial study of community adjustments to changes in river patterns, stereoscopic and digital graphics of ancient bookkeeping all point to processes of human ingenuity and creativity. It is as if we are asserting once again the primacy of community and individual worth in human history and prehistory.

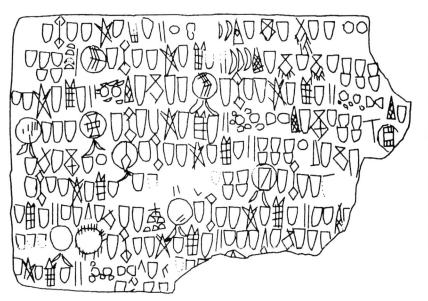

94
Thomas Wight Beale, 1985
Computer-generated drawing
Proto-Elamite tablet

Working from stereo-photographs (fig. 92), Beale applies photogrammetry to produce computer drawings of the five-thousand-year-old clay tablets. These graphics expose variations in the depth and direction of incisions into the clay, coming that much closer to the handwriting of the ancient scribes. Lines that **are actually uneven in the tablet and computer graphic are presented in straight alignment in the hand-drawn version (fig. 93), in which the various renderings of individual characters (such as the star and the inscribed circle) are also standardized, losing their idiosyncratic nature.**

95
Henry B. T. Somerville, 1893–1894
Albumen print
New Georgian youths, Solomon Islands

An officer in the British Royal Navy's great hydrographic survey of the Pacific, Somerville made informal reports based on his observations of the local peoples, using *Notes and Queries on Anthropology* as his guide. Published by the Royal Anthropological Institute of Great Britain and Ireland (2d ed. 1892), the book assisted travellers and ethnographic observers in collecting and recording information on peoples encountered in foreign lands.

Social and Cultural Anthropology: Responses and Responsibility in the Photographic Encounter

Unless we can record with film and tape the sights and sounds of their life, the world loses— and loses forever—part of the rich repertoire of the past on which we must depend to understand the future.

Margaret Mead, 1969
"Introduction," *Gardens of War*

Photography spread with unbelievable speed through the colonial world of the nineteenth century. By the end of the 1840s some Maori in New Zealand had already faced the camera (King 1985). At first attracted by the more formal and exotic aspects of other cultures, such as costume and ritual, ethnologists later documented the commonplace and intimate as well. Moving from the posed to the spontaneous, from the public to the personal, anthropologists increasingly stressed human similarity rather than exotic diversity. This development brought to the fore the problems of invasion and intrusiveness that had been implicit from the beginning.

Today the social or cultural anthropologist has more recording aids in the field than ever before, including sophisticated photographic apparatus, tape recorders, and video and film equipment. At the same time, and perhaps because of the plethora of technical means available, fieldworkers must be more sensitive to the potential intrusiveness of their information-gathering devices and more aware that how they use the camera is as important as whether it is used at all. After more than a century of ethnographic photography, the ethical dilemmas inherent in the enterprise remain unresolved.

Colonial Encounters

As the expansive industrial empires of Western Europe and the United States spread over the globe in an accelerating search for economic resources and markets, they encountered an unexpected diversity of cultures. The discipline of anthropology developed, in part, to make sense of that diversity, and the camera became increasingly useful to the task. By the last two decades of the century a consensus had formed within the industrial nations, a set of assumptions that justified the course of world events by relegating colonized peoples to physical, intellectual, cultural, and moral inferiority. Some harsher spirits would have consigned them to inevitable extinction as well. Milder souls, while unquestioningly accepting Euro-American racial and cultural ascendancy, nonetheless saw the "lower" portions of humanity as educable and worthy of salvation. They argued that it was the "white man's burden" to care for his benighted brethren and to teach them Christianity, democracy, and civilization.

A large body of documentary ethnographic photography was being produced around the globe before the turn of the century. Colonial administrators often performed the task of ethnographers, observing and describing for their governments the customs and characteristics of colonized peoples. Henry B. T. Somerville, a young lieutenant participating in the British Royal Navy's hydrographic survey of the Pacific Ocean between 1889 and 1900, compiled a striking photographic record of the inhabitants of New Georgia in the Solomon Islands (fig. 95). In the United States a number of professional photographers such as William Henry Jackson and John K. Hillers (see figs. 21 and 28), both employed by the U.S. government, and a handful of anthropologists, including the Bureau of American Ethnology's James Mooney, were documenting Indian life in the field.

Posing and Politics

Various theories of social evolution attempted to account for the apparent disparity among the fates of the peoples of the earth. Most measured "progress" by familiar standards (types of technology, complexity of social organization, etc.) along a single ladder of development, from the rudest Savagery through the stages of Barbarism to the highest Civilization; cultures were assigned to the various developmental stages (Morgan 1877; Stocking 1968:110–132). Most

"*It is premature to judge of the value of composite portraits. They are certainly curious and interesting, and many points will occur to the observer of these Indian faces. In a general way, they seem to confirm the results of a close study of the home-life and the various customs, including the most savage rites of war and religion, made by the writer among this family of Indian tribes, by showing them to be a people, intellectual rather than*

ethnology of the previous century was formulated within this intellectual framework and failed to recognize the integrity of peoples in painful transition, struggling to adjust and survive under chaotic conditions. In the post–Civil War United States these assumptions posed a particularly stark dilemma: civilization or extermination for the American Indian?

Few anthropologists of the time more actively promoted assimilation and education for the Native American than did Alice C. Fletcher, one of the Peabody Museum's first ethnologists and a student of the Plains Indian tribes. Fletcher began fieldwork among the Omahas of Nebraska during the 1880s, which saw the floodtide of assimilationist doctrine as public policy in the United States. In 1886 Fletcher asked photographer Jenness Richardson to prepare the first published composite photographs of North American Indians (fig. 96). The purpose of Fletcher's experiment was similar to that of Earnest A. Hooton several decades later (see fig. 52): to establish a visual representation of an ethnic "type" by combining the physical features of a number of individuals. Both researchers read psychological and cultural characteristics into physiological appearances. Fletcher claimed that her composite images confirmed her ethnographic findings that the Dakotas (Sioux) were a people "intellectual rather than brutal, unawakened rather than degraded," with potential "analytical powers of mind" yet untapped (Fletcher 1886:408). The composites thus lent further support to Fletcher's larger political claims that Plains peoples were potentially responsible farmer-citizens (Mark 1980:67–69). Still, the technique remained tangential to her other field methods, and in contrast to Hooton, Fletcher showed only cautious enthusiasm for such photographic cleverness.

As part of her campaign to demonstrate the Indians' potential for becoming hard-working farm families, for the New Orleans Exposition of 1885 Fletcher arranged a photographic exhibition of Omaha life. To show advances already taken toward white civilization, she presented fairgoers with some well-intentioned assimilationist propaganda. As recent research by historian Joan Mark has shown (n.d.), Fletcher was

FIG. 1.—COMPOSITE FROM PHOTOGRAPHS.   FIG. 2.—COMPOSITE FROM DIRECT SITTINGS.

FIG. 3.—RULING FACE IN FIG. 1.   FIG. 4.—RULING FACE IN FIG. 2.

COMPOSITE PORTRAITS OF THREE DAKOTA WOMEN, SHOWING THE EFFECT OF THE METHOD OF PRODUCTION.

96
Jenness Richardson and Alice C. Fletcher, 1886
Science, **7 May 1886**
Individual and composite photographs of three Dakota (Sioux) women

In Fletcher's first composite photograph (top left), portraits of three individual women were combined. For the second (top right), the same three women sat for a combined portrait exposed on one plate (a triple exposure). Each process revealed a different "ruling" type (bottom left and right): one individual face that seemed to dominate the other two in the composite. This apparent inconsistency demonstrates the unreliability of this kind of photographic "evidence." Although uncertain about their ultimate scientific value, Fletcher did assert that these photographs revealed the untapped intellectual potential in Native Americans.

brutal, unawakened rather than degraded. The
portraits indicate the stamp of tribal fixity,
and reveal the unconsciousness within the individ-
ual of the analytical powers of mind by which man
masters nature,—a peculiarity which is the key to
much in Indian sociology and religion."

Alice C. Fletcher, 1886
"Composite Portraits of American Indians"

97
Hamilton, commissioned by Alice C. Fletcher,
1885
Albumen print
"The tent when set up, the Indian man in full
regalia and the wife seated at the tent door"
Omaha Indians, Nebraska

At the request of the U.S. Commissioner of Education, Fletcher set up a photographic exhibit at the 1885 New Orleans Exposition. Entitled "Indian Civilization," the display featured the Omaha Indians of Nebraska. Fletcher commissioned and carefully staged the sixteen photographs in the exhibit. They included "before" (seen here) and "after" shots, intended to illustrate the Omaha tribe's gradual transformation into a community of peaceful agrarians with "civilized" values and practices (Mark n.d.).

Fletcher was a strong advocate of assimilation for the Native American and played an important role in the passage of the Dawes Act in 1887, an attempt to transfer commonly held tribal lands to individual Indian ownership.

particularly anxious to suggest visually that traditional Omaha family life was monogamous and patriarchal in a sense acceptable to Victorian Americans. Commissioning photographs with strict instructions regarding their content, Fletcher filled them with misleading visual evidence in an attempt to win public sympathy for the Omahas. The apparently monogamous couple in figure 97, for example, is posed in a manner acceptable to the white viewer. The man stands, looking dominant and proprietary; his seated wife appears subservient. In fact, the tent and its paraphernalia, in Omaha culture, are hers. The solitary tent seems to suggest nuclear family life, but again appearances are deceiving. The tent has been erected for the photographic occasion in a farmyard by itself, not as part of the traditional full tribal circle, and in winter, the wrong season for tenting (ibid.:13). In figure 98, white viewers saw two apparently unrelated women engaged in a cooperative food-storage task. Omahas would have assumed, probably more correctly, that these were two wives of the same man, working for the benefit of their shared household (ibid.:12). By carefully staging her scenes visually and withholding verbal explication, Fletcher was able to convey her intended messages without actually lying to her audience. She moved the camera into an ethnographic "field" purposely contrived to teach specific lessons.

In a related context, new Indian and Black students were photographed on arrival at the Hampton Institute in Virginia and again some weeks or months later. The institute was founded on the belief that "black and Native Americans were 'dependent' or 'undeveloped' races who might, with proper training, eventually meet white 'standards' of industry, thrift, and sobriety" (Guimond 1982:5). A record of these "before-and-after" images was compiled in order to demonstrate both the educability of Native and Afro-Americans and the success of the institute's program. Collected by institutions such as the Peabody Museum, these images—although not taken for anthropological purposes—made their way into the professional community. In one photograph (fig. 99), "Carrie Anderson," "Annie Dawson," and "Sarah Walker" (their Indian names were not recorded

for posterity) sit glumly on the floor, wrapped in reservation blankets, in their first hours at Hampton. Fourteen months later (fig. 100), they appear in the clothing of white young ladies, seated at tables and chairs, with the accoutrements of feminine civilization: a book, a doll, and a checkerboard. The Hampton photographs point out the critical relationship between positioning of images and accompanying text in creating meaning for the viewer. The individual photographic biography stood in microcosm for the ascent and improvement of the race, graphically illustrating the progress from tribal barbarism to civilized domesticity.

98
Hamilton, commissioned by Alice C. Fletcher, 1885
Albumen print
"Sod dwelling and . . . the rack on which the braided ears of corn were hung to dry, preparatory to storage for winter use,"
Omaha Indians, Nebraska

"For some forty years the avowed aim of the Hampton Institute has been the training of its pupils for leadership among their people. . . . And the fruits of its labors are seen in some of the younger leaders upon the reservations and in the schools. Such an one is Anna Dawson Wilde, an Arickaree, field matron at Fort Berthold, whose work among the Indian women has made for their progress in wholesome living."

"Indian Leadership"
The Southern Workman
March 1912

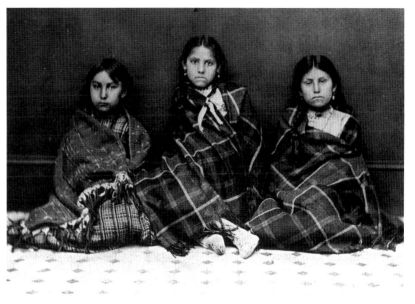

99
Photographer unknown, ca. 1880s
Albumen print
"On arrival at Hampton, Va.: Carrie Anderson—12 yrs., Annie Dawson—10 yrs., and Sarah Walker—13 yrs."

100
Photographer unknown, ca. 1880s
Albumen print
"Fourteen months after," Hampton, Virginia

Between 1878 and the early 1920s, the Hampton Institute in Virginia brought Native American children to the East for education and "civilizing."

Before-and-after photographs of the students recorded the process of assimilation and served to publicize the work of the school.

Photographic Manipulation

At the World's Columbian Exposition in 1893, Frederic Ward Putnam brought groups of native peoples from various parts of the western hemisphere to camp on the Midway of the Chicago fairgrounds during the summer months, manufacturing artifacts and displaying ethnic lifeways. Franz Boas, Putnam's assistant and an early ethnographer of the Kwakiutl, had charge of a village representing the Northwest Coast peoples. Boas and Putnam hired Chicago photographer John H. Grabill to record various Kwakiutl dances (fig. 101), arguing to the fair's administrators that copies of the photographs could be profitably sold to visitors and promising copies to the Kwakiutl dancers and singers as well (Jacknis 1984:6).

Boas has been considered a pioneer of ethnographic photography, but he favored the verbal over the visual in his anthropology. The great weakness of photography, to his mind, was its representation of the frozen moment at the expense of historical depth of understanding (Jacknis 1984:44–45). Boas himself demonstrated, albeit unintentionally, the validity of this criticism. In 1897 he published some of Grabill's photographs of the posed dancers in *The Social Organization and Secret Societies of the Kwakiutl Indians*. Some were retouched. In one image (fig. 102) all but the central figure was removed, and the background was painted to appear naturalistic, as if the photograph had been taken on location in the Northwest. The particularly intrusive "Leather and Shoe Trades" building and the blanket backdrop disappeared along with the row of singers in the background. As visual anthropologist Ira Jacknis has pointed out in his study of these two images (1984), Boas did not consistently indicate such retouching and painting or identify his photographic sources. In this instance, at

least, he utilized photography in a conscious attempt to dismiss the actual historical moment in favor of an idealized "ethnographic present."

Boas's efforts to erase civilization's mundane leather-and-shoe backdrop in order to enhance a scene of Native American ritual bear some reflection. The concentration on, or preference for, formally ritualized aspects of culture reflected the assumption of Boas's generation that ritual contained distilled history and cultural wisdom, that it was the most conservative and thus the most meaningful remnant of culture. More informal, intimate aspects of Kwakiutl life often escaped Boas's camera, if not his awareness. But why photograph a staged performance rather than an actual ritual event? In part the technological limitations of photography still made it necessary to pose or enact ritual. Most of the Kwakiutl dances would be performed at night by firelight, a set of conditions beyond the recording ability of nineteenth-century cameras. In addition, Boas's informants were often performing rituals no longer practiced in the 1890s. They recreated the remembered "original" forms in a generous attempt to assist the ethnographer. Photography was the perfect tool to aid in the manufacture of this dubious product. Boas's efforts to capture, or recapture, a pristine pre-Columbian condition made it difficult for him to appreciate the processes of cultural adjustment occurring before his eyes (cf. Blackman 1980:73).

"We learn from the data of ethnology that not only our ability and knowledge but also the manner and ways of our feeling and thinking is the result of our upbringing as individuals and our history as a people. To draw conclusions about the development of mankind as a whole we must try to divest ourselves of these influences, and this is only possible by immersing ourselves in the spirit of primitive peoples whose perspectives and development have almost nothing in common with our own."

Franz Boas, 1889
"The Aims of Ethnology"

101
John H. Grabill, 1893
Gelatin silver print
Kwakiutl Indian David Hunt dancing as a
hamatsa, World's Columbian Exposition, Chicago

In the summer of 1893, Franz Boas brought Kwakiutl Indians from the Northwest Coast to the World's Columbian Exposition in Chicago to perform dances and ceremonials for the European-American public. Posed in front of a group of singers and a white sheet backdrop that blocked out most of the Exposition background,
David Hunt danced as a hamatsa (cannibal). When Boas later published the picture (1897:plate 28), he retouched the Grabill photograph, erasing the singers and original setting and adding a painted background (fig. 102). Failure to indicate such alterations may confuse the historical and ethnographic record.

DANCE OF THE HĀ'MATS'A.

102
John H. Grabill, 1893, retouched by Franz Boas, 1897
The Social Organization and Secret Societies of the Kwakiutl Indians, 1897
"Dance of the hā'mats'a. . . . From a photograph"

Trait List Photography in Africa

Introduced in the 1880s, Kodak's flexible roll film and portable camera were only the first of several innovations that simplified photography for the nonprofessional. By World War I the camera had become standard gear for social and cultural anthropologists heading for the field. Furthermore, the ethnographic interests of anthropology had begun to converge with the technical abilities of photography. Between 1890 and 1920 theoretical changes led to a deemphasis on cultural decline and greater attention to cultural persistence. As salvage of disappearing cultures faded as a prime motive, the anthropologist began to record the everyday and mundane (in addition to the formally ritualized) in order to understand the sources of cultural continuity and cohesion.

This increased appreciation of living societies expanded the camera's potential as a field tool. Ethnological photography in the twentieth century has shown that the camera can be used with widely varying degrees of aesthetic sensibility and scientific precision. The early work of George Schwab among the Bassa, a Bantu-speaking people of Cameroon, West Africa, is a case in point. A Presbyterian missionary who lived in Africa for fifty years with his wife, Jewell (fig. 103), Schwab emerged after the First World War as "a top-drawer amateur of anthropology," according to Earnest Hooton (Schwab 1947:vii). As a research associate for the Peabody Museum, he became an important contributor to its ethnographic and photographic collections.

Schwab's field photographs taken between 1920 and 1922 show the influence of the trait list school in vogue among American anthropologists between the two world wars, which attempted to outline culture areas by compiling lists of traits—the "minimal definable cultural elements" (De Waal Malefijt 1974:176) — of the culture under study. This approach grew out of the museum context and its associated collecting and cataloguing of cultural items. Schwab seems to have used his camera as a tool to collect data about cultural traits. His imagery was usually determined solely by the information he sought and was sorted into standard anthropological categories: food, shelter, ceremonial objects, handicrafts, methods of manufacture, dress and adornment, entertainment, and physical types. He directed the viewer's attention to the subject at hand by means of pragmatic, rather than aesthetic, portrayals and framing. The visual results were occasionally bizarre (fig. 104), but the discipline with which Schwab used his camera points to a professional rather than a public audience.

Schwab photographed the Bassa as he found them—most of the time, that is. His subjects never appear to have been dressed up or deliberately staged, but his pictures of occupations and daily life activities have little animation. The people seem frozen, possibly at Schwab's direction or because of the camera's intrusion (fig. 105), but other factors also may have played a role. Schwab's exposures were relatively short, so the limitations of technology do not explain the stasis in much of his visual record. "Struggle for a fishhook" (fig. 106) shows that Schwab could employ his camera unobtrusively and demonstrates its capacity to freeze movement. His images may indicate that the aesthetic convention of posing subjects for the camera persisted in anthropology long after photographic technology made it unnecessary.

The Bassa themselves, or their response to Schwab and his intentions, may be partly responsible for their portrayal. In his later ethnographic study of the peoples of Liberia (undertaken in 1928; published in 1947), Schwab encountered "the fear people everywhere had of giving any sort of information on any subject. 'It might be told the Government' and thus, in some unforeseen way, bring trouble upon them" (Schwab 1947:ix). Similar mistrust might easily have contributed to the deadpan approach of the Bassa to the camera. They were careful to reveal nothing about themselves, and perhaps with good reason. Schwab was, after all, a missionary first, an agent of culture change, and the Bassa might reasonably have been expected to keep themselves carefully masked in his presence.

"In 1928 Mrs. Schwab and I set out to make an anthropological survey of the most important tribal groups before their cultures were broken down, to determine what elements in these cultures should be fostered and developed, to study the various problems of readjustment necessary for life under new conditions, and to appraise the mission work among the tribes observed."

George Schwab, 1947
Tribes of the Liberian Hinterland

103
Photographer unknown, ca. 1920
Black-and-white negative
George and Jewell Schwab in canoe on the Nyong River, Cameroon

The Schwabs served as missionaries in Africa for most of the early twentieth century. Although not professionally trained as an anthropologist, George Schwab was affiliated with the Peabody Museum for over thirty years as a research associate in African anthropology. As was true of many early ethnographers, he had a dual role in the field. His ethnography may be evaluated in light of his primary purpose as a missionary and agent of culture change.

104
George Schwab, 1921
Black-and-white negative
Ankle bracelets on Bassa women, Cameroon

Schwab's methodical attention to traits and material culture frequently led him to photograph only the single piece of data he was after, with no particular concern for aesthetics, technical quality, or ethnographic context.

105
George Schwab, 1920–1922
Black-and-white negative
Bassa women in stream, Cameroon

On some occasions Schwab's subjects seemed to "freeze" in front of the photographer, either in response to Schwab's direction (still a common photographic convention among both amateur and professional photographers) or simply to the presence of the camera itself.

106
George Schwab, 1920–1922
Black-and-white negative
Struggle for a fish hook, Cameroon

At other times, albeit infrequently, Schwab did capture the vitality of his subjects.

"Change, anthropology, and history have brought me to the conclusion that anthropology is not a social or behavioral science but a humanistic philosophy."

Cora Du Bois, 1980
"Some Anthropological Hindsights"

"A Clean Eye and an Open Mind"

The photographs taken by Cora Du Bois (fig. 107) during her 1937–1939 fieldwork on the island of Alor in Indonesia (then the Netherlands East Indies) contrast sharply with Schwab's visual record of ethnographic traits. Du Bois looks more to people than to material objects, seeing them as complex social and psychological beings engaged in everyday behavior: eating, sleeping, working, playing, participating in ceremonial events. Her camera moves around easily within these contexts, recording the lives of the people of Alor with intimacy and affection (fig. 108).

Du Bois, a member of the Radcliffe College faculty from 1954 to 1969, was one of the first anthropologists to bring depth psychology and psychoanalytic theory to bear on ethnographic fieldwork. As an undergraduate, she was exposed to the "personality-and-culture" school of anthropology, which investigated the social shaping of personality and the relationships between cultures and the psychology of their members (Benedict 1934). After graduate training, Du Bois began a collaboration with Abram Kardiner, a neo-Freudian (Du Bois 1980). Kardiner developed the concept of a "basic personality structure" in every culture, produced through child-rearing practices including breast-feeding, weaning, and early sexual training—what he called "primary institutions" (Kardiner 1939). In her Alor fieldwork, Du Bois paid particular attention to these practices, augmenting traditional ethnography with dreams, children's drawings, and individual biographies (Du Bois 1944; De Waal Malefijt 1974:307–308).

In order to record relationships and interactions with the camera, Du Bois found it necessary to make photographic sequences, just as primatologists have begun to do more recently in their behavioral studies (see fig. 54). She was in communication with others who were using similar field methods, notably Gregory Bateson and Margaret Mead, whose photographic intentions in *Balinese Character* (1942) were considerably more ambitious. Like Schwab, Du Bois seems to have employed photography simply as a re-

107
Photographer unknown, 1939
Black-and-white negative
Cora Du Bois, Alor, Netherlands East Indies
(Indonesia)

The observer observed
by local children.

cording device, an appropriate means to her own ends. In anthropological training at the time, she later recalled, "it was assumed that your interests were more intellectual and not technical. It was assumed that you would learn the techniques requisite to your problems as you went along. It was assumed also that a clean eye and an open mind were the best equipment for a young field worker" (Du Bois 1966:17). Du Bois focused her "clean eye and open mind" on the raising of an Alor child named Padafan. In one photographic sequence (fig. 109), Padafan begs for a balloon and, to the great amusement of the surrounding children, attempts to nurse from it, throwing a tantrum when it is temporarily taken away.

Du Bois's research centered on a remote mountain community. The people, although aware of more developed coastal settlements, were essentially isolated and protected from the outside world. "No one was exploiting them," Du Bois remarks (1985: personal communication). "We

had a remarkably amiable relationship." During her stay with the Alorese, Du Bois says she began to feel as though she was part of the community, and the Alorese in turn became accustomed to being photographed. The people were pleased when they saw photographs of themselves, she remembers, but were not aware of the uses to which photography could be put and therefore did not pay it much attention.

In general, the Alorese show remarkably easy adaptation to the presence of the camera (fig. 110). It is accepted as an extension, like a pencil or notepad, of Du Bois as observer and participant. Du Bois's camera was the small, unobtrusive, 35mm Leica, but her own lack of self-consciousness probably was also a determining factor in the easy spontaneity of her photographs. To an observer whose interests were understanding another culture from the inside and who could establish a bond with those she studied, a tribal people presented a familiar face.

108
Cora Du Bois, 1939
Black-and-white negative
Wolmaoe and her small sister sleeping on verandah in mid-morning, Alor, Indonesia

Du Bois made her photographic record of life on the island of Alor before the disruptions of World War II. Her photographs, most of which remain unpublished, present close-up views of virtually every aspect of Alor social life.

109
Cora Du Bois, 1939
Black-and-white negative
Behavior sequence of a child, Alor, Indonesia

An interest in behavior and psychology led to the use of sequential photography in social and cultural anthropology, an example of theory determining photographic method. In this series, Du Bois recorded the actions and expressions of the child Padafan as he begs for a balloon, tries to nurse from it, and screams with rage at its removal. Du Bois saw in this "free play episode" a demonstration of the psychological intensity focused on food and the mild teasing and infantile jealousy often associated with the weaning process in Alorese society (Du Bois 1944:41—41).

110
Cora Du Bois, 1938
Black-and-white negative
Elders watch Padafan and other children play at lego-lego, a traditional circle dance.
Alor, Indonesia

Du Bois's nonintrusive photographic equipment, her "amiable" relationship with the people, and the easy adaptation of the Alorese to the camera reduced the psychological distance between photographer, subject, and viewer of the images.

Scanning Settlements from the Air

The Second World War, like the First, gave enormous impetus to aerial photography for military reconnaissance and the global search for natural resources. Social and cultural anthropologists, whose "participant observation" methodology generally involved close personal contact with native peoples, did not adopt aerial survey techniques as readily as did archaeologists. The concerns of ethnology were not usually expressed in terms that made such survey seem useful. Between 1945 and 1960, however, renewed interest in the relationships between human behavior and environment resulted in the development of several schools of "cultural ecology," notably that of Julian Steward of Columbia University. Concern with the environmental determinants of cultural patterns spawned efforts to view contemporary human settlements in broader geographical and topographical scope. The obvious place to do so was from the air.

In 1957 anthropologist Evon Z. Vogt founded the Harvard Chiapas Project, which he has directed for nearly thirty years. He centered his attention on Zinacantan, one of twenty-one Tzotzil-speaking municipalities in the highlands of southeastern Mexico, a region that is the home of some two hundred thousand Maya Indians. Here the Indians maintain the settlement pattern of the ancient Maya: political-religious ceremonial centers surrounded by outlying hamlets. On the assumption that "this settlement plan evolved early in Mayan cultural history and that the Mayas have tended to follow it in essence ever since," Vogt asked the question: Is this continuity a function of ecological conditions or inherited cultural patterns (Vogt 1974:63)? More broadly, Vogt undertook basic ethnographic studies in order to trace the trends of social and cultural change in the highlands and predict the impact of future contact with the industrialized world.

As one phase of the Chiapas project, Vogt began in 1963 an ambitious aerial photography survey (Vogt, ed. 1974). The project surveyed 6,400 square miles of the highlands from high altitudes (13,000 to 18,000 feet above the surface) with a combination of cameras. The RC-9, a wide-angle mapping camera with a curved film plane, was used to take more than a thousand exposures during the first season, with a large amount of overlapping to permit stereoscopic viewing (fig. 111). In addition, a 70mm high-acuity scanning camera took panoramic pictures of nearly 1,000 square miles of designated areas, from which Vogt and his students and colleagues assembled photomosaics of the region (fig. 112). Over the years these have been studied repeatedly by anthropologists and native informants for information regarding settlement patterns, land tenure, markets, communication routes, and the sacred geography of the region. Vogt has commented that "the major mountaintop shrines show up clearly in the photographs, and with the aid of informants we were able to pinpoint the shrines at the foot of the mountains as well as the location of sacred caves on the sides of the mountains" (Vogt 1974:67). This information was an essential part of Vogt's study of Zinacantecan religious and ceremonial life in *Tortillas for the Gods* (1976).

While helping to paint a detailed picture of Zinacantecan life, the Chiapas aerial photographs have been valuable for census-taking, investigating long-range cycles of ecological change, and suggesting new avenues for ethnographic research (Vogt 1974:76–77). Thus, while the ethnographer's camera on the ground may reveal the details of daily life, from the sky the scanning eye of the camera collects information that places human activities in historical and regional contexts. Distance does not ensure objectivity or lack of intrusiveness, as the Santo Domingo incident discussed earlier so forcefully reveals. The technological ability (by means of aerial photography or telephoto lenses) to observe people without their consent or even their knowledge can be abused too easily. Aerial photography can be used productively, however, with the cooperation of those being studied and in the framework of a broader ethnological undertaking.

"The first problem faced by the field-worker in any new field situation is the definition of his role. What do you tell 'the natives' you are doing in their community? How do they perceive your strange, intruding presence?"

Evon Z. Vogt, 1978
Bibliography of the Harvard Chiapas Project

111
Compañía Mexicana Aerofoto, S.A., 1964
Pair of black-and-white aerial stereophotographs
Ceremonial center, Zinacantan, Chiapas, Mexico

With the assistance of native informants, anthropologists use aerial stereophotographs to locate sacred shrines and other local landmarks and map the social and sacred geography of the area. Aerial stereophotographs can be made by a twin-lens camera or (as here) created by timing the interval between exposures to produce an overlapping mosaic, revealing hidden features of the landscape.

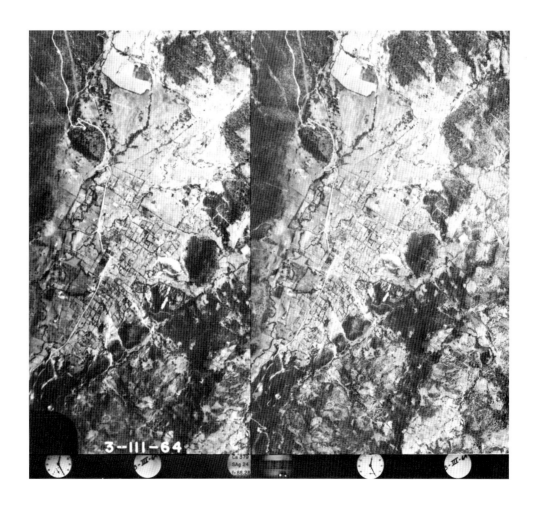

112
Compañía Mexicana Aerofoto, S.A., 1964
Black-and-white aerial photomosaic
Ceremonial center, Zinacantan, Mexico

Composed of dozens of overlapping aerial photographs taken with the 70mm high-acuity (HyAc) scanning camera, photomosaics have been used by the Harvard Chiapas Project for mapping and analyzing settlement patterns, census-taking, mapping land use and land ownership, studying sacred geography, and charting cultural change. The use of aerial photographs saves a great deal of research time, facilitates large-scale ecological analysis, and in some instances provides more precise ethnographic data than conventional field methods.

"Immediate Communication": With the Nomads in Afghanistan

As recently as the Second World War many peoples of the earth inhabited separate, even isolated, worlds. While many anthropologists were constrained by conscience in deciding which images to publish at home, there was little concern about the pictures or the attitudes they engendered returning to the subjects and disrupting their lives. In our smaller, highly interdependent world—precisely because the investigator possesses such powerful tools of modern imagery and communication—trust and respect must be at the heart of the anthropological relationship.

The ethnographic photography of Thomas Barfield (fig. 113), recording his 1975–1976 fieldwork among the nomadic Central Asian Arabs of northeastern Afghanistan, illustrates contemporary field relationships. His work has become especially poignant since the Soviet invasion of Afghanistan in 1979, when the mountains and pastures he photographed became scenes of warfare. Many of the people in his pictures either have fled or been killed. Barfield, a social anthropologist at Harvard, and his collaborator, Donna Wilker, documented the nomads' annual migration from the lowland Amu Dar'ya River valley to the high mountain pastures of Badakhshan in May and June (Barfield 1981).

The nomads migrate seasonally, spending spring on the steppe, summer in the mountains, and fall and winter in the river lowlands. The summer migration takes about three weeks, covering one hundred fifty miles of rugged terrain and a rise in altitude of ten thousand feet. During mid-August, after pasturing their sheep in the mountains during the summer months, the nomads watch for Sirius, "the cold star," to appear on the horizon and signal their return to the valley pastures.

113
Gorm Pedersen, 1975
Color transparency
Thomas Barfield in nomads' winter camp, Afghanistan

Wearing typical Afghan dress, except for the wire-rim glasses that give him away as a foreigner, Thomas Barfield sits with his hosts on the sleeping platform of a reed yurt in *qishloq* (winter camp).

"Part of being an anthropologist is that you must invade people's lives. It is a matter of mutual trust."

Thomas Barfield, 1985

Barfield's visual record is both a stimulus to memory and a repository of information for future study. By recording the everyday aspects of nomad life, Barfield preserved a wealth of ethnographic data, far more than could be recorded by an individual observer using nonphotographic methods. His photograph of a bazaar (fig. 114)—showing the height of the walls, different types of animals offered for sale, individuals present, costumes, gestures, facial expressions—helps the ethnographer recall the scene in all its detail and provides additional data for observation and interpretation. The photographs also convey to the viewer a vivid sense of direct experience. The migration shots (figs. 115–118) have a dazzling visual richness that may surpass verbal description in its sensory impact, although photography can never supplant the written word in terms of explicating meaning. "There is an immediacy in having recognizably real people in their day-to-day activities," remarks Barfield. Photography "captures a way of life that is immediately communicated" (1985: personal communication). For students of anthropology and the wider public, such visual imagery may help engender a respect for the rhythmic integrity of all cultures.

Since Afghanistan has historically served as a trading nexus between East and West, nomads have participated for generations in an international conflux of cultures and have developed a

114
Thomas Barfield, 1975
Color transparency
Animal bazaar, Imam Sahib, Afghanistan

Photography can record aspects of everyday life that otherwise may not be recalled, such as the details of this animal bazaar (*bazaar-i-gosfan*) in the Amu Dar'ya River valley.

115
Donna Wilker, 1976
Color transparency
Migration from winter settlement to mountains, Afghanistan

Migration to the mountains begins in late May and lasts three weeks. Disruptions in Afghan life brought about by the current war may have forever altered the ancient rhythms of nomadic life.

116
Thomas Barfield, 1976
Color transparency
Nomad girl collecting camel dung, Afghanistan

After the nomads tra-
verse the first mountain
passes, firewood be-
comes scarce and dung
is used for cooking
fires. Although a zoom
lens could bring the
subject closer to the

viewer, many social and
cultural anthropolo-
gists, concerned that
their subjects be aware
that they are being
photographed, eschew
the use of long-focal-
length lenses.

cosmopolitan awareness. Barfield found that the
Afghan nomads were sophisticated about cameras and photography, and they had quite definite social boundaries regarding their use.
Many of the nomad men had been photographed
in studios in the city. The formality of the studio portrait suited their sense of the perma-
nence of an image: they posed with unsmiling
dignity, preferably displaying a watch and a
gun. Even in casual situations, Afghans would
adopt a somewhat formal pose (fig. 119). The
Afghans raised few objections to Barfield's photography, but insisted that the pictures of Afghan women be shown only in other parts of the
world, never in Afghanistan. Their culture is
sex-segregated: women did not begin to meet
openly with Barfield until Wilker joined him in
the field, and only a woman was permitted to
photograph other women.

Barfield acknowledges the difficulties anthropologists face as they invade the lives of others.
Many fieldworkers choose not to use the camera
because it can create additional distance between researcher and subject. Others are reluc-
tant to employ photography because they want
to be regarded in the field as scientists rather
than tourists. What is crucial, Barfield believes
(1985: personal communication), is not the
presence or absence of the camera itself, but a
relationship of trust and familiarity that allows
for its successful use.

117
Thomas Barfield, 1976
Color transparency
Migration from winter settlement to mountains,
Afghanistan

The migration contin-
ues. Male heads of
households commonly
ride stallions, placing
their wives and chil-
dren on mares and
their unmarried daugh-
ters on loaded camels.

The narrow, treacher-
ous mountain trails,
however, sometimes
dictate that the men
walk or ride the more
sure-footed mares.

118
Thomas Barfield, 1975
Color transparency
Nomads' summer settlement, Afghanistan

A nomad shepherd makes a fire near his stone shelter in the mountains, away from the main summer settlement (*ailoq*). Later he will return to the main camp and another will replace him to tend the sheep.

119
Thomas Barfield, 1973
Color transparency
Posed portrait of a nomad, Afghanistan

Barfield found that nomad men, many of whom were familiar with photography and cameras, preferred posed portraits in which they could control the image they presented.

The Shavante: Making Deals with Modernity

Ethnographic photography serves not only as a recorder of cultural metamorphosis, but sometimes as a measure of change as well. In 1958, and during several return visits in the 1960s, Harvard anthropologist David Maybury-Lewis and his wife, Pia, lived in central Brazil among the Shavante Indians, a hunting-and-gathering people with a reputation as fierce and hostile warriors. The Shavante came into contact with Euro-Americans in the early 1950s, and Maybury-Lewis described their first encounter with metal fishhooks, bullets, tape recorders, and the camera (Maybury-Lewis 1965). Using a 35mm camera and black-and-white film, the Maybury-Lewises captured scenes of male initiation rites while the Shavante were still relatively unfamiliar with the camera and Western culture (figs. 120 and 121).

In 1982 the Maybury-Lewises returned to the Shavante to examine the effects of twenty years of Western contact. William Crawford, a professional photographer, accompanied them to illustrate the changes and to "learn what I could about how people from preliterate societies look at photographs and respond to being photographed" (Crawford 1983:52). Photographic technology had improved since 1958, but the Shavante had changed too (Crawford 1985: personal communication):

> The Indians had all seen photographs and many owned photographs of themselves or of members of their families. Yet I found that they were often uncomfortable when a camera was around, far more uncomfortable than David had remembered from two decades before. Now they made it clear that they would only be photographed as they wanted to see themselves, at their best, in their best modern clothes, but still looking like Shavante.

The strong warrior tradition among the Shavante encourages public visibility and display by males in dancing, body-painting, and presentation in councils. The same characteristic dance postures recorded by the Maybury-Lewises in

120
David Maybury-Lewis, 1958
Black-and-white negative
Chief Abowa prepares a Shavante boy
for initiation into manhood. Rio das Mortes,
Pimental Barbosa, southeast Mato Grosso, Brazil

Maybury-Lewis carried a 35mm camera at the time of his early fieldwork among the Shavante of central Brazil, but he feels that photographic and other technological equipment can be "intensely alienating" and may inhibit good ethnographic relationships. He says that "for short visits," he now prefers to "disassociate myself from photography altogether" (Maybury-Lewis 1985: personal communication).

1958 were visible to Crawford in 1982, accen-
tuated now by red running shorts, a Western
product readily adopted by Shavante males,
who traditionally value running speed as an at-
tribute of warriors (figs. 122 and 123). Crawford
created instant images, which he gave to the
Shavante to encourage them to pose for more
formal portraits (fig. 124). Their reluctance to
be photographed was no match for their desire
to own a photograph. "From the Indians' point
of view, it was an acceptable deal," Crawford
later reflected (1985: personal communication).

121
David Maybury-Lewis, 1958
Black-and-white negative
Shavante boys sit in the initiation hut.
Rio das Mortes, Pimental Barbosa, Brazil

122
David and Pia Maybury-Lewis, 1958
Color transparency
Shavante men dancing, Pimental Barbosa, Brazil

During the initiation of Shavante boys, age-sets of senior men go to the initiation hut at night to sing songs and keep the boys "alert." They then walk through the village, stopping at various points to form a circle and dance. The Shavante disparage "sleepy" villages in which nothing happens at night. Dances such as this may occur at any time, day or night.

123
William Crawford, 1982
Color transparency
Shavante men dancing during a curing ceremony, Pimental Barbosa, Brazil

Today the Shavante style of dancing—singing while holding hands in a circle, shoulders slouching forward—is known throughout Brazil. The telephone line and red running shorts mark the passage of twenty-four years between this picture and Maybury-Lewis's 1958 photograph (fig. 122).

124
William Crawford, 1982
Type C print
**Portrait of a Shavante youth, Areōns, southeast
Mato Grosso, Brazil**

While Shavante women
avoid the camera,
young men are willing
to be photographed,
even proud of their vis-
ibility. But, as is usually
the case when power
relationships permit it,
today they insist on
being taken on their
own terms.

"Making a deal" seems to express the common mode of adjustment in much of the world today. A century ago resistance to photography was usually attributed to superstition and ignorance. It has since become obvious that the deeper issue was always vulnerability: being "exposed" on someone else's terms. As Michael King observed of photography among the Maori, "Once it occurred to Maori that they need not simply be passive subjects for European photographers, that they could order and arrange pictures for their own purposes, they began to look upon the process more favorably" (King 1985:41). As a result, this Western technology was adopted to confirm rather than undermine traditional values.

Intimacy always carries with it a burden of respect and responsibility (Hinsley 1981:199), and photographic intimacy, which involves a special exposure of human lives, adds a special need for sensitivity. But this is a concern of fairly recent origin. The transition from the large box camera to the 35mm, from close-up to long-distance and aerial photography, has drastically reduced the material intrusiveness of the ethnographic camera and increased the ease of photography. Anthropologists can now probe ever more closely into people's lives. At the same time, increased awareness on the part of both anthropologists and native peoples may open new avenues for communicating visually from one culture to another (fig. 125).

125
Valerie General, Patrick Green (photographers),
and Yvonne Maracle (designer), 1985
Gelatin silver print
"Visions"

Native Americans have become involved in expressing their point of view through the photographic medium. Through exhibition, publication, and public **forums, the Native Indian/Inuit Photographers' Association in Ontario, Canada, is working to foster the use of photography by native peoples.**

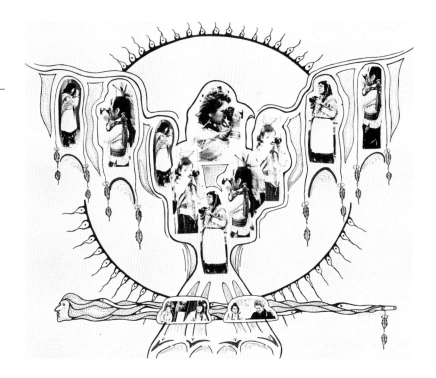

126
Robert Gardner, 1985
Color transparency
Workers at a sand factory, Harishchandra Ghat,
Benares (Varanasi), India

The Eyes that Look Back at Us

Since man must be known through being closely observed by another of his own kind, be a creature with the same basic characteristics and potentials, the success or failure of anthropology is largely a question of the discriminative power of each investigator.

Robert Gardner, 1958
"Anthropology and Film"

In a fragile, politically splintered world, we need to see each other clearly. Otherwise, as Columbus wrote (Major 1870:16), "all is mere conjecture" and hearsay abounds. On a planet made smaller by the omnipresence of global telecommunications, photography wields more influence than ever before and carries heavier ethical burdens. Because the ethical issues are not inherent in the technology itself but derive from its uses, the impact of photography depends less on the camera than on the person standing behind it.

The power of photography is real. All the dreams of its early enthusiasts were exceeded long ago. Whether pondering the skull of *Siva-pithecus*, microanalyzing an Iron Age knife, or studying an Alorese child's activity, we are able through the use of photography to expand the scope of our investigations and understanding. And photographs themselves have become increasingly important as evidence, vital to the preservation and analysis of vanishing cultural resources.

Photography has been witness to the interaction of human beings in an uncertain venture—the attempt to know ourselves through studying others. Historically, the interaction between anthropologist and subject has reflected the political contexts in which the discipline has

developed, and its results often were formulated as a measure against which people were compared and judged. By revealing the attitudes, frustrations, and hopes of participants on both sides of this encounter, the photograph may allow us to see that people in other times and places are not so dissimilar. Apparent differences are valuable expressions of a rich diversity in the human spirit. We turn to the photograph to discover something fundamental about anthropology and ourselves.

127
Photographer unknown, ca. 1890s
Albumen print
Edward H. Thompson with native "guide,"
Yucatán, Mexico

Bibliography

Adams, Richard E. W., W. E. Brown, Jr., and T. Patrick Culbert
1981   "Radar Mapping, Archeology, and Ancient Maya Land Use."
        Science 213(4515):1457–1463.

Agassiz, Elizabeth C., and Louis Agassiz
1868   *A Journey in Brazil*. Boston: Ticknor and Fields.

Ahern, Wilbert H.
1983   "'The Returned Indians': Hampton Institute and its Indian
        Alumni, 1879–1893." *Journal of Ethnic Studies* 10(4):101–
        124.

Alaska, Division of State Libraries and Museums
1981   *A Guide to Historical Photographs in the Alaska State Library*.
        Juneau: Alaska Department of Education, Division of State Li-
        braries and Museums.

Alonso, Mary Ellen, ed.
1979   *China's Inner Asian Frontier: Photographs of the Wulsin Expedi-
        tion to Northwest China in 1923*. Cambridge: Peabody Mu-
        seum, Harvard University.

American Heritage
1977   "On the Whole, He'd Rather Not Be in Philadelphia." *Ameri-
        can Heritage* 28(6):110.

American Journal of Photography
1858   "Editorial Miscellany." Seely's *American Journal of Photogra-
        phy* 1:82 (1 August 1858). In *Photography in American*, W.
        Welling, 1978:129. New York: Thomas Y. Crowell Company.

Anthropological Society of Paris
n.d.   *Photographs of Racial Types*. 6 vols. *Chinese and Japanese;
        Arabs, Turks, Jews and Persians; Europeans, Gypsies, Hindoos
        and Egyptians; Negroes and Sundries; Plaster Casts from Na-
        ture; Cochin Chinese and Siamese*. Tozzer Library, Harvard
        University.

Asad, Talal, ed.
1973   *Anthropology and the Colonial Encounter*. London: Ithaca
        Press.

Asch, Timothy, John Marshall, and Peter Spier
1973   "Ethnographic Film: Strucure and Function." In *Annual Review
        of Anthropology* 2:179–187. Palo Alto, California: Annual Re-
        views Inc.

Bacon, Edward, ed.
1976   *The Great Archaeologists*. London: Secke and Warburg.

Banta, Melissa
1980   "Photographic Archives Computerization Project, Peabody Mu-
        seum, Harvard University." *Studies in the Anthropology of Vis-
        ual Communication* 8(3):9–11.
1982   "Hidden Treasures: The Peabody Museum Photo Archives."
        Views 3(4):8–10; 30.

Barfield, Thomas J.
1981   *The Central Asian Arabs of Afghanistan: Pastoral Nomadism in
        Transition*. Austin: University of Texas Press.
1983   "Nomads." *Symbols* (Fall):10–13.

Barthes, Roland
1981   *Camera Lucida: Reflections on Photography*. New York: Hill
        and Wang.

Barnouw, Victor
1979   *Anthropology: A General Introduction*. Homewood, Illinois: The
        Dorsey Press.

Bateson, Gregory, and Margaret Mead
1942   *Balinese Character: A Photographic Analysis*. New York Acad-
        emy of Sciences, Special Publications 2. New York: New York
        Academy of Sciences.

Beals, Ralph L.
1982   "Unity and Diversity in Anthropology." In *Crisis in Anthropol-
        ogy*, ed. E. A. Hoebel, R. Currier, and S. Kaiser, 51–64. New
        York and London: Garland Publishing.

Benedict, Ruth
1934   *Patterns of Culture*. Boston and New York: Houghton Mifflin.

Bevan, Bruce
1975   "An Introduction to Stereo Photography." In *Photography in
        Archaeological Research*, ed. E. Harp, Jr., 259–263. Albu-
        querque: University of New Mexico Press.

Bishop, Ralph
1985   "Stones, Bones, and Margaret Mead: The Image of American
        Anthropology in the General Press, 1927–1983." *Anthropology
        Newsletter* (April):18–19.

Blackman, Margaret B.
1976   "Blankets, Bracelets, and Boas: The Potlatch in Photographs."
        Anthropological Papers of the University of Alaska 18(2):53–67.
1980   "Posing the American Indian: Early Photographers Often
        Clothed Reality in Their Own Stereotypes." *Natural History*
        89(10):68–75.
1981   *Window on the Past: The Photographic Ethnohistory of the
        Northern and Kaigani Haida*. Canadian Ethnology Service, Pa-
        per 74. Ottawa: National Museum of Canada.
1982a   "'Copying People': Northwest Coast Native Response to Early
        Photography." In *The Past in Focus: Photography and British
        Columbia, 1858–1914*, ed. J. M. Schwartz, 86–112. B.C.
        Studies, Special Issue 52.
1982b   "The Afterimage and Image After: Visual Documents and the
        Renaissance in Northwest Coast Art." *American Indian Art*
        7(2):30–39.
1986   "The Studio Indian: Documenting Archival Photographs from
        British Columbia." *Archivaria* 21 (forthcoming).

Boas, Franz
1889   "The Aims of Ethnology." In *The Shaping of American Anthro-
        pology, 1883–1911: A Franz Boas Reader*, ed. G. H. Stocking,
        Jr., 67–71. New York: Basic Books.
1897   *The Social Organization and the Secret Societies of the Kwakiutl
        Indians*. Report of the U.S. National Museum 1895:311–737.
        Washington, D.C.: Government Printing Office.
1932   "The Aims of Anthropological Research." *Science* (n.s.)
        76:605–613.
1940   *Race, Language and Culture*. New York: Macmillan.

Bowditch, Charles P.
n.d.   Collected Papers. Peabody Museum Archives. Cambridge: Har-
        vard University.

Brace, C. Loring
1982   "The Roots of the Race Concept in American Physical Anthro-
        pology." In *A History of American Physical Anthropology,
        1930–1980*, ed. F. Spencer, 11–29. New York: Academic
        Press.

Brain, Jeffrey P.
1979   *Tunica Treasure*. Peabody Museum of Archaeology and Ethnology, Papers 71. Cambridge: Peabody Museum, Harvard University.

Brew, J. Otis
1966   *People and Projects of the Peabody Museum, 1866–1966*. Cambridge: Peabody Museum, Harvard University.

Brinton, Daniel G.
1895   "The Aims of Anthropology." *Appleton's Popular Science Monthly* 48(1):59–72.

Byers, Paul
1966   "Cameras Don't Take Pictures." *Columbia University Forum* 9(1):27–33.

Capper, Colonel J.E.
1907   "Photographs of Stonehenge, as seen from a War Balloon." *Archaeologia* 60(2): plates 69 and 70.

Carmichael, Elizabeth
1973   *The British and the Maya*. London: The British Museum.

Carnegie Institution of Washington, D.C.
1929   "Colonel and Mrs. Lindbergh Aid Archaeologists. Part I—The Aerial Survey of the Pueblo Region." *News Service Bulletin* (Staff Edition) 18:109–113.
1937   "Copan—G. Stromsvik." *Annual Report of the Division of Historical Research, Yearbook 36* (1936–1937):3–5.

Catherwood, Frederick
1844   *Views of Ancient Monuments in Central America, Chiapas, and Yucatan*. London: F. Catherwood.

Ceram, C. W.
1951   *Gods, Graves, and Scholars. The Story of Archaeology*. New York: Alfred A. Knopf.

Charnay, Désiré
1862–   *Cités et ruines américaines: Mitla, Palenqué, Izamal, Chichen-
1863   Itza, Uxmal, receuillies et photographiées par Désiré Charnay avec un texte par M. Viollet-le-Duc*. 2 vols. Paris: Gide.

Chicago, World's Columbian Exposition, 1893
1894   *Oriental and Occidental, Northern and Southern Portrait Types of the Midway Plaisance; a Collection of Photographs of Individual Types of Various Nations from all Parts of the Department of Ethnology, the Manners, Customs, Traits and Peculiarities of their Race*. Introduction by Prof. F. W. Putnam. Educational Art Series. 2 vols. St. Louis: N. D. Thompson Publishing Co.

Collier, John Jr.
1957   "Photography in Anthropology: A Report on Two Experiments." *American Anthropologist* (n.s.) 59:843–859.
1967   *Visual Anthropology: Photography as a Research Method*. New York: Holt, Rinehart and Winston.

Conlon, V. M.
1973   *Camera Techniques in Archaeology*. New York: St. Martin's Press.

Cookson, Maurice B.
1954   *Photography for Archaeologists*. Foreword by Sir Mortimer Wheeler. London: Max Parrish.

Crawford, Osbert Guy Stanhope, and Alexander Keiller
1928   *Wessex from the Air*. Oxford: Clarendon Press.

Crawford, William
1979   *The Keepers of Light. A History and Working Guide to Early Photographic Processes*. New York: Morgan and Morgan.
1983   "The Shavanti of Central Brazil." *Polaroid* 14(1):52–53.

Daniel, Glyn E.
1950   *A Hundred Years of Archaeology*. London: G. Duckworth and Co.

Davis, Keith F.
1981   *Désiré Charnay, Expeditionary Photographer*. Albuquerque: University of New Mexico Press.

Deuel, Leo
1969   *Flights into Yesterday; the Story of Aerial Archaeology*. New York: St. Martin's Press.
1978   *Memoirs of Heinrich Schliemann: A Documentary Drawn from his Autobiographical Writings, Letters, and Excavation Reports*. London: Hutchinson.

Deuel, Leo, ed.
1961   *The Treasures of Time*. Cleveland: The World Publishing Co.

DeVore, Irven
1963   "Comparative Ecology and Behavior of Monkeys and Apes." In *Classification and Human Evolution*, ed. S. L. Washburn, 301–319. Chicago: Aldine.

DeVore, Irven, ed.
1965   *Private Behavior: Field Studies of Monkeys and Apes*. New York: Holt, Rinehart and Winston.

De Waal Malefijt, Annemarie
1974   *Images of Man: A History of Anthropological Thought*. New York: Alfred A. Knopf.

Dexter, Ralph W.
1966   "Putnam's Problems Popularizing Anthropology." *American Scientist* 54(3):315–332.
1976   "The Role of F. W. Putnam in Developing Anthropology at the American Museum of Natural History." *Curator* 19(4):303–310.

Diamond, Stanley
1980   "Anthropological Traditions: The Participants Observed." In *Anthropology: Ancestors and Heirs*, ed. S. Diamond, 1–16. The Hague: Mouton.

Dommash, Hans L., and the Mendal Art Gallery
1979   *The Silver Image: A History of Photography, 1839–1970*. Saskatoon, Saskatchewan: Saskatoon Gallery and Conservatory Corporation.

Du Bois, Cora
1944   *The People of Alor: A Social-Psychological Study of an East Indian Island*. Minneapolis: University of Minnesota Press.
1966   "Ethnography and Social Science," Vice-Presidential Address read at Annual Meeting of the American Association for the Advancement of Science, Washington, D.C., 29 December.
1980   "Some Anthropological Hindsights." *Annual Review of Anthropology* 9:1–13. Palo Alto, California: Annual Reviews Inc.

Earle, Edward W.
1981   "Vision Machinery: New Applications for Videodisc Technology." *Afterimage* 8(9):4.

Eimerl, Sarel, and Irven DeVore
1965   *The Primates*. New York: Time-Life Books.

Ellul, Jacques
1964   *The Technological Society*. Translated by John Wilkinson. New York: Knopf.

Fagan, Brian M.
1984   "Archaeology and the Wider Audience." In *Ethics and Values in Archaeology*, ed. E. L. Green, 175–183. New York: The Free Press.

Fagin, Nancy L.
1984   "Closed Collections and Open Appeals: The Two Anthropology Exhibits at the Chicago World's Columbian Exposition of 1893." *Curator* 27(4):249–264.

Ferrez, Gilberto, and Weston J. Naef
1976   *Pioneer Photographers of Brazil, 1840–1920*. New York: Center for Inter-American Relations.

Fisk, Harold, N.
1944   *Geological Investigation of the Alluvial Valley of the Lower Mis-
       sissippi River. War Department, Corps of Engineers, U.S. Army.*
       Washington, D.C.: Mississippi River Commission, Publication
       52.

Fletcher, Alice C.
1885a *Historical Sketch of the Omaha Tribe of Indians in Nebraska.*
       Washington, D.C.
1885b *The Indian Bureau at the New Orleans Exposition; Report of
       Alice C. Fletcher to the Honorable Commissioner of Indian Af-
       fairs.* Washington, D.C.
1886   "Composite Portraits of American Indians." *Science*
       7(170):408–409.

Gaede, Marc, and Marnie Gaede
1980   *Camera, Spade and Pen: An Inside View of Southwestern Ar-
       chaeology.* Tucson: University of Arizona Press.

Galassi, Peter
1981   *Before Photography: Painting and the Invention of Photogra-
       phy.* New York: Museum of Modern Art.

Gardner, Robert
1958   "Anthropology and Film." *Daedalus* 86(4):344–352.

Gardner, Robert, and Karl G. Heider
1969   *Gardens of War: Life and Death in the New Guinea Stone Age.*
       New York: Random House.

Gaucheraud, H.
1839   "The Fine Arts: A New Discovery." *La Gazette de France*
       (Paris), 6 January 1839. In *Photography: Essays and Images,*
       ed. B. Newhall, 1980:17. New York: Museum of Modern Art.

Gavin, Carney E. S.
1978   "Bonfils and the Early Photography of the Near East." *Harvard
       Library Bulletin* 26:442–470.
1982   *The Image of the East; Nineteenth-Century Near Eastern Photo-
       graphs by Bonfils from the Collections of the Harvard Semitic
       Museum.* Chicago: University of Chicago Press.
1985   "Photo-Archaeology and Tomorrow's Museums: Fragile Links of
       Silver to the Sunlight of Our Past." *Museum* 145:5–12.

Gavin, Carney E. S., Elizabeth Carella, and Ingeborg O'Reilly
1981   "The Photographers Bonfils of Beirut and Alès 1867–1916."
       Camera (March).

Geertz, Clifford J.
1973   "Thick Description." In *The Interpretation of Cultures,* 3–30.
       New York: Basic Books.

Gerlach, S. Craig, Margaret B. Blackman, and Edwin S. Hall, Jr.
1985   *Custodians of the Past: The North Slope Borough Field School.*
       Edwin Hall and Associates, Technical Memorandum 19.

Gidley, Mick
1979   *With One Sky Above Us: Life on an Indian Reservation at the
       Turn of the Century.* New York: Putnam.

Glenn, James R.
1981   "'The Curious Gallery': The Indian Photographs of the McClees
       Studio in Washington, 1857–1858." *History of Photography*
       5:249–262.
1983   "De Lancey W. Gill: Photographer for the Bureau of American
       Ethnology." *History of Photography* 7(1):7–22.

Goldschmidt, Walter R., ed.
1979   *The Uses of Anthropology.* Washington, D.C.: American An-
       thropological Association.

Gordon, George Byron
1896   *Prehistoric Ruins of Copan, Honduras. A Preliminary Report of
       the Explorations by the Museum, 1891–1895.* Peabody Museum
       of American Archaeology and Ethnology, Memoirs 1(1). Cam-
       bridge: Peabody Museum, Harvard University.

1902   *The Hieroglyphic Stairway, Ruins of Copan. Report on Explora-
       tions by the Museum.* Peabody Museum of American Archaeol-
       ogy and Ethnology, Memoirs 1(6). Cambridge: Peabody
       Museum, Harvard University.

Gould, Stephen Jay
1981   *The Mismeasure of Man.* New York: Norton.

Graham, Ian
1971   *The Art of Maya Hieroglyphic Writing.* Cambridge: Peabody
       Museum, Harvard University.
1977   "Alfred Maudslay and the Discovery of the Maya." *The British
       Museum Yearbook II: Collectors and Collections:* 137–155. Lon-
       don British Museum Publications.
n.d.   "Catalogue for Planned Maler/Maudslay Exhibition." Peabody
       Museum, Harvard University. Typescript.

Graham, Ian, gen. ed.
1975– *Corpus of Maya Hieroglyphic Inscriptions.* 11 fascicles. Cam-
       bridge: Peabody Museum, Harvard University.

Green, Ernestene L., ed.
1984   *Ethics and Values in Archaeology.* New York: The Free Press.

Guimond, James
1982   "'The Vanishing Red': Native Americans in Frances Johnston's
       Hampton Album." Department of English, Rider College.
       Typescript.

Hallowell, A. Irving
1965   "The History of Anthropology as an Anthropological Problem."
       Journal of the History of Behavioral Sciences 1:24–38.

Harp, Elmer, Jr., ed.
1975   *Photography in Archaeological Research.* Albuquerque: School
       of American Research, University of New Mexico Press.

Harvard University Library
1984   *Photographs at Harvard and Radcliffe: A Directory.* Cambridge:
       Harvard University Library.

Haworth-Booth, Mark
1984   *The Golden Age of British Photography, 1839–1900.* Millerton,
       New York: Aperture.

Hencken, Hugh
1978   *The Iron Age Cemetery of Magdalenska gora in Slovenia.*
       Mecklenburg Collection, Part II. American School of Pre-
       historic Research, Bulletin 32. Cambridge: Peabody Museum,
       Harvard University.

Hencken, Hugh, ed.
1968   *Data on Iron Age Horses of Central and Eastern Europe* by S.
       Bökönyi and *Human Skeletal Material from Slovenia* by J. L.
       Angel. Mecklenburg Collection, Part I. American School of
       Prehistoric Research, Bulletin 25. Cambridge: Peabody Mu-
       seum, Harvard University.

Hinsley, Curtis M., Jr.
1980   "Archives of the Peabody Museum of Archaeology and Ethnol-
       ogy, Harvard University." *History of Anthropology Newsletter*
       7(2):3–4.
1981   *Savages and Scientists: The Smithsonian Institution and the De-
       velopment of American Anthropology, 1846–1910.* Washington,
       D.C.: Smithsonian Institution Press.
1985   "Hemispheric Hegemony in Early American Anthropology,
       1841–1851: Reflections on John Lloyd Stephens and Lewis
       Henry Morgan." In *Social Contexts of American Ethnology,
       1840–1984,* ed. J. Helm, 28–40. Washington, D.C.: American
       Anthropological Association.

Hinsley, Curtis M., Jr., and Bill Holm
1976   "A Cannibal in the National Museum: The Early Career of
       Franz Boas in America." *American Anthropologist* 78(2):306–
       316.

Hockings, Paul, ed.
1975   *Principles of Visual Anthropology.* The Hague: Mouton.

Hodgen, Margaret T.
1964   *Early Anthropology in the Sixteenth and Seventeenth Centuries.* Philadelphia: University of Pennsylvania Press.

Hoebel, E. Adamson, Richard Currier, and Susan Kaiser
1982   *Crisis in Anthropology; View from Spring Hill, 1980.* New York and London: Garland Publishing.

Holmes, Lowell D., ed.
1972   *Readings in General Anthropology.* New York: Ronald Press.

Hooton, Earnest A.
1930   *The Indians of Pecos Pueblo. A Study of their Skeletal Remains.* New Haven: Yale University Press.
1931   *Up from the Ape.* New York: Macmillan.
1937a   *Apes, Men, and Morons.* New York: G. P. Putnam's Sons.
1937b   "What Shall We Do To Be Saved?" *Harvard Alumni Bulletin* (5 March):650–656.
1939   *Crime and the Man.* Cambridge: Harvard University Press.
1940   *Why Men Behave like Apes and Vice Versa.* Princeton: Princeton University Press.
1942   *Man's Poor Relations.* Garden City, New York: Doubleday, Doran and Company.
1951   *Handbook of Body Types in the United States Army (White Males).* 2 vols. Department of the Army. Office of the Quartermaster General. Military Planning Division. Research and Development Branch. Environmental Protection Section.

Hooton, Earnest A., and Frederick L. Stagg
1953   "Body Build and Life Record of 2631 Harvard Alumni of the Classes 1884–1912." Tozzer Library, Harvard University. Typescript.

Huizer, Gerrit, and Bruce Mannheim, eds.
1979   *The Politics of Anthropology: From Colonialism and Sexism Toward a View from Below.* The Hague: Mouton.

Hrdlička, Aleš
1920   *Anthropometry.* Philadelphia: Wistar Institute of Anatomy and Biology.

Hymes, Dell, ed.
1973   *Reinventing Anthropology.* New York: Random House.

International Center of Photography
1984   *Encyclopedia of Photography.* New York: Crown Publishers.

Jacknis, Ira
1984   "Franz Boas and Photography." *Studies in the Anthropology of Visual Communication* 10(1):2–60.

Johnson, Rossiter, ed.
1898   *History of the World's Columbian Exposition, Held in Chicago in 1893.* Vol. 2: "Departments." New York: D. Appleton.

Kardiner, Abram
1939   *The Individual and His Society: The Psychodynamics of Primitive Social Organization.* New York: Columbia University Press.

Kerston, Lincoln
1966   *The Hampton Album.* New York: Museum of Modern Art.

Kidder, Alfred V.
1929   "Colonel and Mrs. Lindbergh Aid Archaeologists. Part II—The Aerial Survey of the Maya Region." Carnegie Institution of Washington, D.C., *News Service Bulletin* (Staff Edition) 19:115–121.
1930   "Five Days over the Maya Country." *Scientific Monthly* (March):193–205.

King, Michael
1985   "Maori Images." *Natural History* 7(85):37–43.

Kroeck, Richard M.
1966   *A Manual for Users of Aerial Photography of the Highlands of Chiapas, Mexico.* Vidya Report 233. Palo Alto, California: Vidya.

Lamberg-Karlovsky, C. C., and Piero Meriggia
n.d.   "The Proto-Elamite Tablets from Tepe Yahya." Department of Anthropology, Harvard University. Typescript.

Layard, Austen Henry
1849   *Nineveh and its Remains.* London: John Murray.

Le Plongeon, Augustus
1886   *Sacred Mysteries among the Mayas and the Quiches, 11,500 Years Ago. Their Relation to the Sacred Mysteries of Egypt, Greece, Chaldea and India. Free Masonry in Times Anterior to the Temple of Solomon.* New York: Secret Doctrine Reference Series. Minneapolis: Wizards Bookshelf 1973.

Lewis, Diane
1973   "Anthropology and Colonialism." *Current Anthropology* 14(5):581–602.

Longo, Donna
1980   "Photographing the Hopi." *Pacific Discovery* 33(3):11–19.

Lurie, Edward
1960   *Louis Agassiz: A Life in Science.* Chicago: University of Chicago Press.

Lyman, Christopher
1982   *The Vanishing Race and Other Illusions: Photographs of Indians by Edward S. Curtis.* New York: Pantheon Books.

Major, Richard Henry
1870   *Select Letters of Christopher Columbus, with Other Original Documents Relating to His Four Voyages to the New World.* 2d ed. London: Hakluyt Society.

Maler, Teobert
1901–   *Researches in the Central Portion of the Usumatsintla Valley;*
1903   *Reports of Explorations for the Peabody Museum (1897–1900).* Peabody Museum of American Archaeology and Ethnology, Memoirs 4(1). Cambridge: Peabody Museum, Harvard University.
1908   *Explorations in the Department of Peten, Guatemala and Adjacent Region: Topoxté; Yāxhá; Benque Viejo; Naranjo; Reports of Explorations for the Museum.* Peabody Museum of American Archaeology and Ethnology, Memoirs 4(2). Cambridge: Peabody Museum, Harvard University.
1910   *Explorations in the Department of Peten, Guatemala and the Adjacent Region: Motul de San José; Peten-Itza; Reports of Explorations for the Museum.* Peabody Museum of American Archaeology and Ethnology, Memoirs 4(3). Cambridge: Peabody Museum, Harvard University.
1911   *Explorations in the Department of Peten, Guatemala: Tikal.* Peabody Museum of American Archaeology and Ethnology, Memoirs 5(1). Cambridge: Peabody Museum, Harvard University.

Mark, Joan T.
1980   *Four Anthropologists: An American Science in its Early Years.* New York: Science History Publications.
n.d.   "Photography as Propaganda: The Indian Bureau Exhibit at the New Orleans Exposition in 1885." Peabody Museum, Harvard University. Typescript.

Marshack, Alexander
1972   *The Roots of Civilization: The Cognitive Beginnings of Man's First Art, Symbol and Notation.* New York: McGraw-Hill.

Masayesva, Victor, Jr., and Erin Younger
1983   *Hopi Photographers, Hopi Images.* Tucson: Sun Tracks.

Massachusetts Board of World's Fair Managers
1894   *Report of World's Columbian Exposition.* Boston: State Printer.

Maudslay, Alfred P.
1899–   *Archaeology. Biologia centrali-americana.* 5 vols. London: Porter and Dulan and Co.
1902

Maybury-Lewis, David
1965   *The Savage and the Innocent.* Cleveland and New York: The World Publishing Company.

Mead, Margaret
1968   "Introduction." In *Gardens of War*, R. Gardner and K. Heider,
        vii–x. New York: Random House.
1975   "Visual Anthropology in a Discipline of Words." In *Principles
        of Visual Anthropology*, ed. P. Hockings, 3–10. The Hague and
        Paris: Mouton.

Meltzer, David J.
1983   "The Antiquity of Man and the Development of American Ar-
        chaeology." *Advances in Archaeological Method and Theory*
        6:1–51.

Metz, Charles
n.d.   Collected Papers. Cincinatti: Cincinatti Historical Society.

Morgan, Lewis Henry
1877   *Ancient Society, or Researches in the Lines of Human Progress
        from Savagery, through Barbarism to Civilization*. New York:
        Henry Holt and Company.

Morley, Sylvanus Griswold
1920   *The Inscriptions at Copan*. The Carnegie Institution of Wash-
        ington, Publication 219. Washington, D.C.: Carnegie Institu-
        tion.
1937–   *The Inscriptions of Peten*. Carnegie Institution of Washington,
1938   Publication 437. Washington, D.C.: Carnegie Institution.
1943   "Archaeological Investigations of the Carnegie Institution of
        Washington in the Maya Area of Middle America, During the
        Past Twenty-Eight Years." *Proceedings of the American Philo-
        sophical Society* 86(2):205–218.

Morrison, Philip, and Phylis Morrison
1982   *Powers of Ten*. San Francisco: W. H. Freeman and Company.

Morton, Samuel George
1839   *Crania Americana, or, a Comparative View of the Skulls of the
        Various Aboriginal Nations of North and South America. To
        which is Prefixed an Essay on the Varieties of the Human Spe-
        cies*. Philadelphia: Dobson.
1844   *Crania Aegyptiaca; or, Observations on Egyptian Ethnography,
        Derived from Anatomy, History, and the Monuments*. Philadel-
        phia: Penington.

Movius, Hallam L., Jr.
1974   "The Abri Pataud Program of French Upper Paleolithic in Ret-
        rospect." In *Archaeological Research in Retrospect*, ed. G. Wil-
        ley, 87–116. Cambridge: Winthrop Press.
1977   *Excavation of the Abri Pataud, Les Eyzies (Dordogne): Stratig-
        raphy*. American School of Prehistoric Research, Bulletin 31.
        Cambridge: Peabody Museum, Harvard University.

Movius, Hallam L., Jr., ed.
1975   *Excavation of the Abri Pataud, Les Eyzies (Dordogne)*. Ameri-
        can School of Prehistoric Research, Bulletin 30. Cambridge:
        Peabody Museum, Harvard University.

Myres, J. L.
1908   "Herodotus and Anthropology." In *Anthropology and the Clas-
        sics*, ed. R. R. Marett, 121–168. Oxford: Clarendon Press.

Nash, Gary B.
1974   *Red, White, and Black: The Peoples of Early America*. Engle-
        wood Cliffs, New Jersey: Prentice-Hall.

Newhall, Beaumont
1964   *The History of Photography*. New York: Museum of Modern
        Art.

Newhall, Beaumont, ed.
1980   *Photography: Essays & Images. Illustrated Readings in the His-
        tory of Photography*. New York: Museum of Modern Art.

Ogleby, Clifford L.
1983   "Form from Old Photos: The Geometric Analysis of Historic
        Photography." *Working Papers on Photography* 9:65–67.

Pagden, Anthony
1982   *The Fall of Natural Man: The American Indian and the Origins
        of Comparative Ethnography*. Cambridge: Cambridge University
        Press.

Peabody Museum of Archaeology and Ethnology
1866   Letterbooks 1:1. Peabody Museum Archives. Cambridge: Har-
        vard University.

Petrie, W. M. Flinders
1902–   *Abydos*. 2 vols. Egypt Exploration Fund, Memoir 22. London:
1903   Egypt Exploration Fund.
1904   *Methods and Aims in Archaeology*. London: MacMillan and Co.

Phillips, Philip
1970   *Archaeological Survey in the Lower Yazoo Basin, Mississippi,
        1949–1955*. Peabody Museum of Archaeology and Ethnology,
        Papers 60. Cambridge: Peabody Museum, Harvard University.

Phillips, Philip, James A. Ford, and James B. Griffin
1951   *Archaeological Survey in the Lower Mississippi Alluvial Valley,
        1940–1947*. Peabody Museum of Archaeology and Ethnology,
        Papers 25. Cambridge: Peabody Museum, Harvard University.

Pilbeam, David
1982   "New Hominoid Skull Material from the Miocene of Pakistan."
        Nature 295(5846):232–236.
1983   "Hominoid Evolution: Harvard's Program and Field Research
        in Pakistan," *Symbols* (Fall):2–3; 14–15.

Poidebard, Antoine
1934   "La trace de Rome dans le désert de Syrie: Le limes de Trajan
        à la conquête arabe, recherches aériennes (1925–1932)." *An-
        tiquity* 8:373–380.

Poignant, Roslyn
1980   *Observers of Man: Photographs from the Royal Anthropological
        Institute*. London: Royal Anthropological Institute.

Powell, Walter Clement
1948–   "Journal of W. C. Powell, April 21, 1871–December 7, 1872,"
1949   ed. Charles Kelly. In *The Exploration of the Colorado River
        and the High Plateaus of Utah by the Second Powell Expedition
        of 1871–72. Utah Historical Quarterly* XVI–XVII:257–478.

Putnam, Frederic Ward
1890   "The Serpent Mound of Ohio." *Century* 39(6):871–888.
1894   "Introduction." In *Portrait Types of the Midway Plaisance*, Chi-
        cago, World's Columbian Exposition, 1893. St. Louis: N. D.
        Thompson Publishing Co.
1973   *The Archaeological Reports of Frederic Ward Putnam, Selected
        from the Annual Reports of the Peabody Museum of Archaeology
        and Ethnology, Harvard University, 1875–1903*. Antiquities of
        the New World, vol. 8. New York: AMS Press for the Peabody
        Museum, Harvard University.

Reeves, Dache M.
1936   "Aerial Photography and Archaeology." *American Antiquity*
        2(2):102–107.

Reichlin, Elinor T.
1977   "Faces of Slavery." *American Heritage* 28(4):4–5.

Reisner, George
n.d.   Biographical File. Pusey Archives. Cambridge: Harvard Uni-
        versity.

Ribnick, Rosalind
1982   "A Short History of Primate Field Studies: Old World Monkeys
        and Apes." In *A History of American Physical Anthropology,
        1930–1980*, ed. F. Spencer, 49–73. New York: Academic
        Press.

Ricketson, Oliver, Jr., and A. V. Kidder
1930   "An Archaeological Reconnaissance By Air in Central Amer-
        ica." *The Geographical Review* 20(2):177–206.

Ritzenthaler, Mary Lynn, Gerald J. Munoff, and Margery S. Long
1984 *Archives & Manuscripts: Administration of Photographic Collections*. Chicago: Society of American Archivists.

Robl, Ernest H., ed.
1983 *Picture Sources 4*. New York: Special Libraries Association.

Rockett, Will H.
1983 "The Bonfils Story." *Aramco World* 34(6):9–31.

Rosencrantz, Donald M.
1975 "Underwater Photography and Photogrammetry." In *Photography and Archaeological Research*, ed. E. Harp, Jr., 223–263. Albuquerque: University of New Mexico Press.

Rowe, John Howland
1953 "Technical Aids in Anthropology: A Historical Survey." In *Anthropology Today: An Encyclopedic Inventory*, ed. A. L. Kroeber, 895–940. Chicago: University of Chicago Press.

Royal Anthropological Institute of Great Britain and Ireland
1892 *Notes and Queries on Anthropology*. 2d ed. London: The Anthropological Institute.

Rubenstein, Joseph
1981 "Photographic Facts: False Realities." *Dialectical Anthropology* 5(4):341–349.

Rubin, William, ed.
1984 *"Primitivism" in 20th Century Art: Affinity of the Tribal and the Modern*. New York: Museum of Modern Art.

Ruby, Jay
1973 "Up the Zambesi with Notebook and Camera, or Being an Anthropologist without Doing Anthropology...with Pictures." *Society for the Anthropology of Visual Communication Newsletter* 4(3):12–15.
1976 "In a Pic's Eye: Interpretive Strategies for Deriving Significance and Meaning from Photographs." *Working Papers in Culture and Communication* 1(2):22–38.
1980 "Franz Boas and Early Camera Study of Behavior." *Kinesis Report* 3(1):6–11, 16.

Ruby, Jay, ed.
1980 *The Human Condition: A Photographic Exhibition of the 1980 Conference on Visual Anthropology*. Philadelphia: The Philadelphia Art Alliance.
1982 *A Crack in the Mirror: Reflexive Perspectives in Anthropology*. Philadelphia: University of Pennsylvania Press.

Rudisill, Richard
1973 *Photographers of the New Mexico Territory, 1854–1912*. Santa Fe: Museum of New Mexico.

Rydell, Robert W.
1984 *All the World's a Fair: Visions of Empire at American International Expositions, 1876–1916*. Chicago: University of Chicago Press.

St. Joseph, J. Kenneth S., ed.
1966 *The Uses of Air Photography: Nature and Man in a New Perspective*. London: John Baker Publishers.

Saley, Richard, and Thomas Wight Beale
1985 "A New Terrestrial Photogrammetric System for Archaeology: A Progress Report." In *Proceedings of the 1983 Harvard Computer Graphics Conference*, vol. 2. Cambridge: Harvard University Laboratory for Computer Graphics and Spacial Analysis.

Scheil, Vincent, ed.
1923 "Textes de comptabilité proto-Élamites." *Mémoires de la mission archéologique de Perse: Mission en Susiane* 17.

Scherer, Joanna Cohan
1973 *Indians: The Great Photographs that Reveal North American Indian Life, 1847–1929. From the Unique Collection of the Smithsonian Institution*. New York: Crown Publishers, Inc.
1975a "Pictures as Documents: Resources for the Study of North American Ethnohistory." *Studies in the Anthropology of Visual Communication* 2(2):65–66.

1975b "You Can't Believe Your Eyes: Inaccuracies in Photographs of North American Indians." *Studies in the Anthropology of Visual Communication* 2(2):67–79.
1981a "Historical Photographs of the Subarctic: A Resource for Future Research." *Arctic Anthropology* 18(2):1–16.
1981b "Repository Sources of Subarctic Photographs." *Arctic Anthropology* 18(2):59–66.

Schiller, Dan
1977 "Realism, Photography, and Journalistic Objectivity in 19th Century America." *Studies in the Anthropology of Visual Communication* 4(2):86–98.

Schliemann, Heinrich
1880 *Ilios: The City and Country of the Trojans*. London: John Murray.

Schmidt, Erich F.
1940 *Flights Over Ancient Cities of Iran*. Chicago: University of Chicago Press.

Schwab, George
1947 *Tribes of the Liberian Hinterland: Report of the Peabody Museum Expedition to Liberia*, ed. G. W. Harley. Peabody Museum of American Archaeology and Ethnology, Papers 31. Cambridge: Peabody Museum, Harvard University.

Schwartz, Joan M., ed.
1982 *The Past in Focus: Photography and British Columbia, 1858–1914*. B.C. Studies, Special Issue 52.

Sheldon, William H.
1942 *The Varieties of Temperament: A Psychology of Constitutional Differences*. New York: Harper and Brothers.
1954 *Atlas of Men: A Guide for Somatotyping the Adult Male at All Ages*. New York: Harper and Brothers.

Slotkin, Richard L.
1974 *Regeneration Through Violence: The Mythology of the American Frontier, 1600–1860*. Middleton, Connecticut: Wesleyan.

Smith, Harrison W.
1911 "Notes on Tahiti." *National Geographic* 22(11):947–963.
1919 "Sarawak, the Land of the White Rajahs." *National Geographic* 35:110–167.

Smuts, Barbara
1985 *Sex and Friendship in Baboons*. New York: Aldine Publishing.

Sobieszek, Robert, and Carney E. S. Gavin
1980 *Remembrances of the Near East: The Photographs of Bonfils, 1867–1907*. Rochester: International Museum of Photography, George Eastman House and Cambridge: Harvard Semitic Museum, Harvard University.

Sontag, Susan
1970 "The Anthropologist as Hero." In *Claude Lévi-Strauss: The Anthropologist as Hero*, ed. E. N. Hayes and T. Hayes, 184–196. Cambridge: The MIT Press.
1977 *On Photography*. New York: Farrar, Straus and Giroux.

Sorenson, E. Richard
1975 "Visual Records, Human Knowledge, and the Future." In *Principles of Visual Anthropology*, ed. P. Hockings, 463–476. The Hague: Mouton.
1976 *The Edge of the Forest: Land, Childhood and Change in a New Guinea Protoagricultural Society*. Washington, D.C.: Smithsonian Institution Press.

The Southern Workman
1912 "Indian Leadership." *The Southern Workman* 41(3):131–134.

Stanton, William R.
1960 *The Leopard's Spots: Scientific Attitudes Toward Race in America, 1815–1859*. Chicago: University of Chicago Press.

Stephens, John Lloyd
1841 *Incidents of Travel in Central America, Chiapas and Yucatan*. 2 vols. With illustrations by Frederick Catherwood. New York: Harper and Brothers.

1843 *Incidents of Travel in Yucatan*. 2 vols. With illustrations by Frederick Catherwood. New York: Harper and Brothers.

Steward, Julian H.
1939 *Notes on Hillers' Photographs of the Paiute and Ute Indians taken on the Powell Expedition of 1873*. Smithsonian Miscellaneous Collections 98(18). Washington, D.C.: Smithsonian Institution.

Stocking, George W., Jr.
1968 *Race, Culture, and Evolution: Essays in the History of Anthropology*. New York: The Free Press.
1979 *Anthropology at Chicago: Tradition, Discipline, Department*. Chicago: University of Chicago Press.
1983 "History of Anthropology: Whence/Wither." In *Observers Observed: Essays on Ethnographic Fieldwork*, ed. G. W. Stocking, Jr., 3–12. Madison, Wisconsin: University of Wisconsin Press.

Stockly, Walter
1939 "Hooton of Harvard." *Life* 7(6):60–66 (7 August 1939).

Susman, Warren
1984 *Culture as History: The Transformation of American Society in the Twentieth Century*. New York: Pantheon.

Taft, Robert
1938 *Photography and the American Scene: A Social History, 1839–1889*. New York: Dover.

Thomas, Alan
1982 "Photography of the Indian: Concept and Practice on the Northwest Coast." In *The Past in Focus: Photography and British Columbia, 1858–1914*, ed. J. M. Schwartz, 61–68. B.C. Studies, Special Issue 52.

Thompson, Edward Herbert
1888 "Portal at Labna, Yucatan." In *Ancient Yucatan and Mexico*, E. H. Thompson, A. Le Plongeon, and L. H. Ayme, article 3. Worcester, Massachusetts: Press of Charles Hamilton.
1904 *Archaeological Researchers in Yucatan; Reports of Explorations for the Museum*. Peabody Museum of American Archaeology and Ethnology, Memoirs 3(1). Cambridge: Peabody Museum, Harvard University.
1929 "Forty Years of Research and Exploration in Yucatan." *Proceedings of the American Antiquarian Society* 39(1):38–48.
188? "Photographs of Yucatan." Tozzer Library, Harvard University. Portfolio.

Times of London
1985 *The Times, Past, Present, Future*. London: The Times.

Trachtenberg, Alan, ed.
1980 *Classic Essays on Photography*. New Haven: Leete's Island Books.

Vaczek, Louis, and Gail Buckland
1981 *Travellers in Ancient Lands. A Portrait of the Middle East, 1839–1919*. New York: New York Graphic Society (Little, Brown).

Van Dusen, William I.
1930 "Exploring the Maya with Lindbergh." *Saturday Evening Post* (11 January):40, 43, 154, 157–158.

Viola, Herman J.
1974 "North American Indian Photos from the National Anthropological Archives, Smithsonian Institution." Chicago: University of Chicago Press. Microfiche.

Vogt, Evon Z.
1969 *Zinacantan: A Maya Community in the Highlands of Chiapas*. Cambridge: Harvard University Press.
1974 "Aerial Photography in Highland Chiapas Ethnography." In *Aerial Photography in Anthropological Field Research*, ed. E. Z. Vogt, 57–77. Cambridge: Harvard University Press.
1976 *Tortillas for the Gods: A Symbolic Analysis of Zinacanteco Ritual*. Cambridge: Harvard University Press.

1978 *Bibliography of the Harvard Chiapas Project: The First Twenty Years, 1957–1977*. Cambridge: Peabody Museum, Harvard University.

Vogt, Evon Z., ed.
1974 *Aerial Photography in Anthropological Field Research*. Cambridge: Harvard University Press.

von Hagen, Victor Wolfgang
1950 *Frederick Catherwood, Architect*. New York: Oxford University Press.

Washburn, Sherwood L.
1977 "Field Study of Primate Behavior." In *Progress in Ape Research*, ed. G. H. Bourne, 231–242. New York: Academic Press.

Waterfield, Gordon.
1963 *Layard of Nineveh*. New York: Praeger.

Weaver, Thomas, ed.
1973 *To See Ourselves: Anthropology and Modern Issues*. Glenview, Illinois: Scott, Foresman, and Co.

Welling, William
1976 *Collector's Guide to Nineteenth-Century Photographs*. London and New York: Collier Macmillan Publishers.
1978 *Photography in America: The Formative Years, 1839–1900*. New York: Thomas Y. Crowell Company.

Wells, Peter S.
1981 *The Emergence of an Iron Age Economy: The Mecklenburg Grave Groups from Hallstatt and Stična*. Mecklenburg Collection, Part III. American School of Prehistoric Research, Bulletin 33. Cambridge: Peabody Museum, Harvard University.

White, Anne Terry
1941 *Lost Worlds; Adventures in Archaeology*. New York: Random House.

Whittlesey, Julian
1975 "Elevated and Airborne Photogrammetry and Stereo Photography." In *Photography and Archaeological Research*, ed. E. Harp, Jr., 265–309. Albuquerque: University of New Mexico Press.

Williams, Stephen, and Jeffrey P. Brain
1970 *Philip Phillips: Lower Mississippi Survey, 1940–1970*. Cambridge, Peabody Museum, Harvard University.
1983 *Excavations at the Lake George Site, Yazoo County, Mississippi, 1958–1960*. Peabody Museum of Archaeology and Ethnology, Papers 74. Cambridge: Peabody Museum, Harvard University.

Wissler, Clark A.
1923 *Man and Culture*. New York: Thomas Y. Crowell Company.

Worswick, Clark
1979 *Japan. Photographs 1854–1905*. New York: Pennwick Publishing, Inc.

Worswick, Clark, and Ainslie Embree
1976 *The Last Empire: Photography in British India, 1855–1911*. Millerton, New York: Aperture.

Worth, Sol
1976 "Doing Anthropology of Visual Communication." *Working Papers in Culture and Communication* 1(2):2–21.

Worth, Sol, and John Adair
1974 *Through Navajo Eyes: An Exploration in Film Communication and Anthropology*. Bloomington: Indiana University Press.

Wyman, Jeffries
n.d. Collected Papers. Countway Library, Harvard University Medical School. Boston: Harvard University.

Younger, Erin
1983 "Changing Images: A Century of Photography on the Hopi Reservation." In *Hopi Photographers, Hopi Images*, V. Masayesva, Jr., and E. Younger, 13–40. Tucson: Sun Tracks.

Photographic Index

The photographic index provides information on the copyright and/or source for all images appearing in this catalogue. The index also includes photograph numbers and object numbers for materials from the collections of the Peabody Museum, Harvard University. Images followed by an asterisk (*) are copyright by the President and Fellows of Harvard College.

66	N31144 *
67	N285 *
68	N361 *
69	N386 *
70	N31145 *
71	H29-3-37 *
72	H29-3-62 *
73	N31146 © 1930 The Curtis Publishing Company
74	Courtesy U.S. Department of the Interior
75	*
76	N31147 Courtesy U.S. Department of the Interior
77	N31148 *
78	Courtesy Louisiana Office of State Parks
79	N30707 *
80	N31149 *
81	*
82	*
83	*
84	*
85	T781 Courtesy Tozzer Library, Harvard University
86	N29871 Courtesy Peabody Museum
87	N27662 Courtesy Peabody Museum
88	N2117 *
89	H31-1-84 *
90	*
91	© 1975 National Geographic Society
92	© Thomas Wight Beale, Courtesy Musée du Louvre
93	Courtesy Musée du Louvre
94	© Thomas Wight Beale

Chapter 7

95	N31150 Courtesy Peabody Museum
96	N31151 Courtesy Cabot Science Library, Harvard University
97	N31152 Courtesy Peabody Museum
98	N31153 Courtesy Peabody Museum
99	N30439A Courtesy Peabody Museum
100	N30440A Courtesy Peabody Museum
101	N29641 Courtesy Peabody Museum
102	Courtesy Department Library Services, American Museum of Natural History. Neg. No. 2A 12823 (Dance of the Hamatsa). Copy photograph by R. P. Sheridan
103	
104	N6816 *
105	N6897A *
106	N6706 *
107	N6787B *
108	DB 52:11 *
	DB 47:17 *

109	DB 53:32,33; 54:13,14,15,18 *
110	DB 49:30 *
111	*
112	*
113	© Gorm Pedersen
114	© Thomas Barfield
115	© Donna Wilker
116	© Thomas Barfield
117	© Thomas Barfield
118	© Thomas Barfield
119	© Thomas Barfield
120	© David Maybury-Lewis
121	© David Maybury-Lewis
122	© David Maybury-Lewis
123	© William Crawford
124	© William Crawford
125	© Yvonne Maracle

Chapter 8

126	© Film Study Center, Harvard University
127	N31154 *